UNDERSTANDING JENNIFER EGAN

UNDERSTANDING CONTEMPORARY AMERICAN LITERATURE

Matthew J. Bruccoli, Founding Editor

Linda Wagner-Martin, Series Editor

Also of Interest

Understanding Alice McDermott, Margaret Hallissy
Understanding Bharati Mukherjee, Ruth Maxey
Understanding Colson Whitehead, Derek C. Maus
Understanding David Foster Wallace, Marshall Boswell
Understanding Gary Shteyngart, Geoff Hamilton
Understanding John Rechy, María DeGuzmán
Understanding Karen Tei Yamashita, Jolie Scheffer
Understanding Randall Kenan, James A. Crank
Understanding Stewart O'Nan, Heike Paul
Understanding William T. Vollmann, Işıl Özcan

UNDERSTANDING
JENNIFER EGAN

Alexander Moran

THE UNIVERSITY OF
SOUTH CAROLINA PRESS

Published by the University of South Carolina Press
Columbia, South Carolina 29208

www.uscpress.com

Manufactured in the United States of America

30 29 28 27 26 25 24 23 22 21
10 9 8 7 6 5 4 3 2 1

Library of Congress Cataloging-in-Publication Data
can be found athttp://catalog.loc.gov/.

ISBN 978-1-64336-224-3 (hardcover)
ISBN 978-1-64336-225-0 (paperback)
ISBN 978-1-64336-226-7 (ebook)

This book is dedicated to Denise, who could not quite make it to see it published.

CONTENTS

SERIES EDITOR'S PREFACE

The Understanding Contemporary American Literature series was founded by the estimable Matthew J. Bruccoli (1931–2008), who envisioned these volumes as guides or companions for students as well as good nonacademic readers, a legacy that will continue as new volumes are developed to fill in gaps among the nearly one hundred series volumes published to date and to embrace a host of new writers only now making their marks on our literature.

As Professor Bruccoli explained in his preface to the volumes he edited, because much influential contemporary literature makes special demands, "the word *understanding* in the titles was chosen deliberately. Many willing readers lack an adequate understanding of how contemporary literature works; that is, of what the author is attempting to express and the means by which it is conveyed." Aimed at fostering this understanding of good literature and good writers, the criticism and analysis in the series provide instruction in how to read certain contemporary writers—explicating their material, language, structures, themes, and perspectives—and facilitate a more profitable experience of the works under discussion.

In the twenty-first century Professor Bruccoli's prescience gives us an avenue to publish expert critiques of significant contemporary American writing. The series continues to map the literary landscape and to provide both instruction and enjoyment. Future volumes will seek to introduce new voices alongside canonized favorites, to chronicle the changing literature of our times, and to remain, as Professor Bruccoli conceived, contemporary in the best sense of the word.

Linda Wagner-Martin, Series Editor

ACKNOWLEDGMENTS

First, I would like to acknowledge the wonderful support of the editor of the series, Linda Wagner-Martin. From the moment I proposed this book she has been a tireless and brilliant person to work with, and the quality of the *Understanding* series is a testament to her amazing work. I would also like to thank everyone at the University of South Carolina Press. Richard Brown made the application process incredibly clear and easy, and the wonderful acquisitions editor, Aurora Bell, has been a kind, patient, and knowledgeable editor to work with (also, it is hard to know who between her and Linda responds more quickly to emails). I would also like to thank the anonymous reviewers and the copyeditor whose careful reading of my manuscript contributed greatly to any insights people may find in these chapters.

I also owe a debt of gratitude to Matthew Luter for helping this project get off the ground. My deepest thanks go to Edward Jackson, whose constant support, counsel, and willingness to hear me ramble about Egan is perhaps the central reason that this book is publishable. Thank you for everything over the last few years; I cannot really repay you, but I hope the Pokémon themed T-shirt on its way to you will at least partially suffice as thanks.

Thanks must also go to my brother, Pat, who feigns interest better than pretty much anyone I know. And last but not least, thank you to my wife, Bonnie. These pages exist due to your support and evident confusion whenever I express doubt that I will complete something.

The chapter on *The Keep* is derived in part from an article published in *Textual Practice*, 12 September 2018, copyright Taylor & Francis, available online: http://www.tandfonline.com/10.1080/0950236X.2018.1509272.

1

Understanding Jennifer Egan

When Jennifer Egan's novel *A Visit from the Goon Squad* won the National Book Critics Circle Award in 2010, the *LA Times* reported the news as "Egan beats Franzen in National Book Critics Circle's fiction prize." *Goon Squad* went unmentioned in the article's subheading ("the Jennifer Egan work bests Jonathan Franzen's *Freedom*"), and in an even more startling act of elision, the article included an image of Franzen rather than her (Edgar). Although the newspaper apologized and corrected this bizarre oversight—but not before the website *Jezebel* satirized the kerfuffle with the headline "Jonathan Franzen Loses Book Award to Some Lady" (North)—this reporting is indicative of the broader way in which Egan's writing has been discussed until quite recently. For most of Egan's career, her fiction has been treated as a byword for excellence rather than analysis. She is a writer who has been largely absent from discussions of literary trends and been mentioned in footnotes or lists rather than at the center of debates. But, with the overwhelming success of *Goon Squad,* Egan's fiction is slowly becoming more popular across literary studies. However, despite a series of much-lauded works of fiction and a quarter of a century writing nonfiction for the *New York Times Magazine, Understanding Jennifer Egan* is the first book-length study of her work to date.

The *LA Times* piece was not the only controversy in which Egan found herself during the literary awards season. After winning the Pulitzer Prize in 2011, she was interviewed by Julie Steinberg for the *Wall Street Journal*. Steinberg asked her if she felt female writers are treated differently by the press than their male counterparts. In response, Egan briefly referred to the writer Kaavya Viswanathan, who had recently been found to have plagiarized the chick lit authors Sophie Kinsella, Meg Cabot, and Megan McCafferty. Egan's complaint was not that Viswanathan had plagiarized, but that "she had plagiarized very derivative, banal stuff. This is your big first move? These are your models?" She went on to say, "My advice for young female writers would be to shoot high and not cower" (Steinberg). These comments annoyed and angered many, with author Jennifer Weiner being particularly perturbed that Egan appeared to be dismissing all chick lit, and Jamie Beckman glibly asking Egan to "not step on other women as you make your way to the podium." Egan immediately regretted her comment, and later described them as "really stupid, ill-informed, and unfortunate" (Ohlson). Egan was also deeply affected by the accusation of sexism, as this was the type of gender-based dismissal and misrepresentation that she has battled throughout her career. As she discussed with Laura Miller a decade earlier in 2001: "I hate about myself the fact that I tend to model myself consciously after male writers. And I think that's because again there's this association that I'm very suspicious of that somehow men take on the big topics more than women do, which I don't think is necessarily true." Egan also spoke of her frustration with the critical response to her first novel, *The Invisible Circus* (1994), saying, "I'm a woman and it was a story about sisters so there was an immediate assumption that there certainly couldn't be anything very intellectual going on there" (Miller). Egan has challenged such simplistic assumptions about women's writing throughout her career. Furthermore, in their formal experiments and stylistic diversity, her texts also challenge what contemporary fiction can do.

As part of her apology for her comments about chick lit, Egan stated, "I'd like to help find a way to move us beyond the literary/commercial binary, which—like all binaries—is artificial, and therefore inherently misleading" (Ohlson). Indeed, as Egan constantly seeks to position her work between traditions and to challenge simple binaries, she is hard to place within many of the frameworks that have been proposed to understand contemporary literature: New Sincerity, neoliberalism, the Program Era, post-postmodernism, and the relationship between contemporary literature and popular genres. However, her work never definitively settles within any one of these frameworks.[1] That Egan's fiction is an uneasy and troubling fit with her contemporaries means she has remained largely absent in the sea of recent studies that have been released to define the contemporary, and when her fiction is discussed, the focus is almost exclusively on *Goon Squad,* such as in Lee Konstantinou's *Cool Characters: Irony and American Fiction* (2016), or Michael Szalay's chapter in *Neoliberalism and Contemporary Literary Culture* (2017).[2] Her earlier work, however, has not yet received the reappraisal it deserves. *Understanding Jennifer Egan* seeks to correct this record. Here, I offer some foundational readings of Egan's earliest short story collection, *Emerald City,* and propose some theoretical frameworks to analyze her under-studied novels *The Invisible Circus, Look at Me,* and *The Keep.* I discuss *The Invisible Circus* as a text exploring the aftermath of the sixties protest movements; I consider *Look at Me* as capturing the early phases of the surveillance of the population by large technology companies; and I explore *The Keep* as a novel that looks at the Gothic nature of communications technology. In the chapters on *A Visit from the Goon Squad* and *Manhattan Beach,* I summarize the previously offered readings of these works, and also propose some new ways to interpret them: *Goon Squad* as a summary of all of Egan's fiction so far, and *Manhattan Beach* not as a historical novel as it is commonly discussed, but as a pastiche of the United States in the 1940s. In these readings, I aim to offer insight, as well as to inspire debate around the works of this remarkable writer.

Although Egan's fiction does not easily fit within any linear account of contemporary fiction as succeeding postmodernism, that is not to say she does not respond to the theories of the postmodern era. Throughout, I often cite Fredric Jameson's canonical formulations about the postmodern period to demonstrate Egan's distinctions from such concerns, which Adam Kelly succinctly summarizes as: "the death of affect, the loss of history, the fragmentation of the subject, the subsumption of the natural into the cultural, and so on" ("Beginning" 398). In this same article Kelly usefully suggests that when reading her work one should begin critical work by affirming "postmodernism, then," meaning that critics should acknowledge the lessons of the period, without claiming contemporary writers are always responding to this era (415). I use this principle throughout to show the distinction, particularly in regard to concepts of authenticity, pastiche, and historical thinking, between Egan's fiction and the world as described by Jameson and other theorists of the postmodern period. Part of the reason for this is that she constantly switches genres and styles from text to text, making her work difficult to categorize. As Egan herself noted in 2006: "My books are all pretty different from each other—to the point where I'm sometimes told that people are surprised that one person wrote them" (Vida). Similarly, despite regularly extolling the virtues of the writers and texts that have influenced her work, Egan has acknowledged, "I also feel sometimes that I'm not sure exactly what tradition I'm part of" (Miller). In reading Egan, a different literary lineage comes to the fore, as she situates herself as simply part of the history of the novel: "Look at a book like *Tristram Shandy,* which is so crazily experimental in a way we still have yet to match," and also, "How about Cervantes? How crazy is *Don Quixote*?" (Michod). She goes on to highlight that "even nineteenth-century novels, which are supposed to be so staid, they're actually not" (Michod). The point is that postmodern fiction does not have a claim to all formal experiments, and a study of Egan's writing illuminates a broader picture of literary history than is often told. She often cites Edith Wharton, *The House of Mirth* (1905) in particular, as a huge influence, and has written a thoughtful introduction to a recent edition of Wharton's classic, as well as George Eliot's *Middlemarch* (1871). She is also an acolyte of Don DeLillo and introduced DeLillo when he won the National Book Foundation's Medal for Distinguished Contribution to American Letters in 2015 (Egan, "Fiction"). Also among her favorite authors are Robert Stone, Doris Lessing, Shirley Hazzard, Ralph Ellison, and Joyce Carol Oates, a more varied collection of influences than many of her contemporaries would cite ("Top Ten"). This unusual cast of influences is another reason why her works sit uneasily within many of the aforementioned paradigms suggested to define contemporary fiction.

However, she is not completely divorced from her peers. This book also seeks to compare Egan to David Foster Wallace in regard to their respective treatments of the sixties protest era; Colson Whitehead, Michael Chabon, and Jonathan Lethem in terms of genre; George Saunders in connection to the recent wave of historical fiction; and Susan Choi, Dana Spiotta, Christopher Sorrentino, and Rachel Kushner in relation to their depictions of terrorism. Moreover, a focus on Egan does not result in the naming of a new movement, mode, or ideal to define the contemporary; as Egan herself wrote in 2014, "Personally, I could do without any further 'isms' (is anyone actually *drawn* to fiction called 'postmodern'?), but I'm stirred by the question of how novels and short stories will evolve to accommodate and represent our ongoing cultural transformation" ("Introduction: Short Stories" xviii). Egan's work therefore reflects what Andrew Hoberek describes as "the heterogeneity of contemporary fiction," a phrase which captures the diversity of modes, genres, and forms used by writers in recent years (236). Similarly, in *Twenty-First Century Fiction: A Critical Introduction* (2013) Peter Boxall states that "the present is elusive to us, that there is something in the contemporary that remains untimely, intransigent, resistant to critical focus." Accordingly, he does not propose "a stable new critical paradigm" to understand the present (17). Nevertheless, despite existing between any "isms" and not strictly adhering to received critical paradigms, Egan's fiction does have some consistent themes and concerns. The rapid changes wrought by technological advancements are a recurring preoccupation of Egan's—she confesses she is "obsessed with voyeurism and telecommunications" ("The 60s" 639)—particularly the effects of the rapid rise in mass media since the 1960s. The challenge that Egan poses to literary scholars is to find a consistent lens through which to read her varied, untimely, and prescient work. Running through this concern with technological change is an interest in its implications for *authenticity*.

Staged Authenticity

Since the turn of the millennium there have been numerous calls for a return to authenticity and real experience. In 2010 David Shields identified a widespread "reality hunger" in American culture. He proposed a "deliberate unartiness" was the defining feature of contemporary art, meaning it was concerned with not being polished and presented, and that the line between fiction and nonfiction was blurring to the point of being redundant (5). These comments appear to predict the recent rise of autofiction—such as the fiction of Sheila Heti, Ben Lerner, and many others—a genre that Allison Gibbons suggests "narrativize the self not as a game, but in order to enhance the realism of a text" (Gibbons "Postmodernism"). Outside of literary debates, in 2003 David Boyle published a polemic in which he argues that the demand for iterations of authenticity and authentic experiences "derives from the so-called 'cultural creatives' in the USA and the so-called 'inner-directeds' in Europe," essentially meaning marketing executives (15). Boyle also cites the rise of reality television—*Survivor* first aired on May 31, 2000—literary movements like "The New Puritans," and the short-lived film collective *Dogme 95* as all being indicative of this broader cultural valorization of authenticity. But at the heart of Boyle's thesis is a contradiction, one which he does not properly acknowledge: How can someone preplan and manage an image of authenticity? Does not such planning render these products immediately inauthentic? This paradox is precisely what preoccupies Egan's writing. Across her fiction, she looks at how images of authenticity are produced, and she questions the ways in which authenticity effects are staged and managed. To return to Shields, he writes that reality hunger is defined by the "seemingly unprocessed" (3). It is this "seemingly," and the precision with which art and experience can be sculpted to appear unprocessed, that are the focus of much of Egan's fiction. One of the biggest influences on Egan's fiction is Daniel Boorstin's 1961 work *The Image: A Guide to Pseudo-Events in America.* Here, Boorstin argues that the world of the 1960s is characterized by pseudo-events, which he defines as an event that is planned for the purposes of being reproduced (11). In an introduction to a collection of stories about the 1960s, Egan observes, "In the sixties we discovered, as a culture, the thrill of watching ourselves" ("The 60s" 637). She goes on to quote Boorstin, arguing that "the great irony of our technological age is that the phoniness of mediated experience leaves us craving authenticity that only more media can seem to satisfy" (637). This perpetual quest for authentic experience, and the technologies that seek to meet this demand, are constant threads throughout Egan's fiction.

Indeed, scholars routinely note how ideas of authenticity or realness characterize much contemporary American fiction. For instance, in Robert

McLaughlin's definitions of post-postmodernism, the extra "post" denotes how writers of Egan's generation "penetrate through the layers," by which he means the very image culture and mass media that is Egan's focus, and aim "perhaps quixotically, to reconnect with something beyond representation, something extralinguistic, something real" (213). When critics discuss Egan's work, they often suggest that she is trying to access something real or authentic; Wolfgang Funk suggests that "Egan's narrative approach in *A Visit from the Goon Squad* can be read as an attempt to retrace these flickering moments of authenticity" (52). This reading misses the ways that *Goon Squad* instead foregrounds the artifice of each moment. Kelly groups Egan with Saunders, Whitehead, and Wallace as writers who see authenticity as a paradox: "If authenticity can be defined as that which cannot be commodified, then it appears that nothing even remotely public can by now remain authentic" ("The New Sincerity" 202). However, although closer to the truth than Funk's characterization of Egan's fiction as capturing flickers of something real, Kelly's interpretation relies on a narrowly defined concept of authenticity as an existentialist idea of being true to oneself. I contend that Egan's fiction is much more concerned with *experiences of authenticity,* particularly in relation to tourism, technology, genre, and memory. For example, touristic experiences are a central concern in *Emerald City* and in *The Invisible Circus.* Similarly, *The Keep* is about setting up a Gothic hotel and creating an authentic tourist experience. Technology and the vast expansion of image culture in contemporary life are other avenues by which Egan approaches authenticity, a theme which she particularly develops in *Look at Me.* She also delves into the complex relationship genre has with authenticity, given that genre fiction has traditionally been understood as being written for the market and thus lacking in critical distance and artistic autonomy. Egan's writing often thematizes how generic frameworks determine interpretation, particularly in *Look at Me, The Keep, A Visit from the Goon Squad,* and *Manhattan Beach.* Finally, another central theme of Egan's fiction is the authenticity of historical memory. This concern is evident from her very first novel, *The Invisible Circus,* in which the protagonist, Phoebe, is on a quest to discover what happened to her sister, as well as to find an authentic counterculture. Experiences of authenticity, for both characters and the reader, are a unifying concern across her writing. However, as noted above, what Egan is particularly interested in is how authenticity is managed, controlled, and staged. Hence, throughout *Understanding Jennifer Egan* I read her fiction as engaging with what Dean MacCannell names "staged authenticity."

MacCannell, a sociologist of tourism, developed his concept of staged authenticity from Erving Goffman's canonical definitions of the self as a form of performance in *The Presentation of the Self in Everyday Life* (1956). Goffman argues that each person adopts a mask that they present to the world, and that only a few select people are allowed to see their authentic back world—one example is the dressing room only certain people can enter before a show. MacCannell complicates this binary, suggesting that when someone is granted access to this back region, there is no way of ascertaining whether this area is authentic or just another stage—whether it is a place of "staged authenticity." MacCannell defines staged authenticity in relation to tourism: "Touristic consciousness is motivated by its desire for authentic experiences, and the tourist may believe that he is moving in this direction, but often it is very difficult to tell for sure if the experience is authentic in fact" ("Staged" 597). Egan's fiction is full of characters trying to experience something real, something authentic, and then never being quite sure when or if they have reached what they were looking for. To take one example of many, in *The Invisible Circus* Phoebe delights in the idea that when she first arrives in London, she sees "everywhere she look[s]—England." At first, the city lives up to her pre-conceived image as a place containing "tabloid salesmen [who] bellowed headlines around wet stubs of cigars," as well as streets where "red double-decker buses sailed past" (104). But after a week in London "flanked by other tourists" (111) she feels like she has failed to have any authentic experiences, and that she needs to make an undefined "crucial leap" (111). Throughout Egan's fiction there are instances of gradual disenchantment, as characters come to realize that experiences they had taken to be authentic have in fact been managed or staged. Indeed, numerous characters are explicitly invested in the management of authenticity, from "The Stylist" in her earliest collection to Scotty Hausmann' in the dramatic performance that concludes *Goon Squad*. To be clear, at stake in her fiction is not the successful representation of authenticity, or even "flickers of authenticity"—in fact, part of her point is that it is impossible for fiction to represent authenticity, as she asserts that fiction writing "is all artificial" (Dinnen "Artificial"). She is not attempting to get to "something real," as McLaughlin notes, but to show how characters manage and sculpt images of such. This dovetails with how MacCannell defines staged authenticity: "Staged authenticity does not involve authenticity in any philosophical register. It only involves the putative removal of barriers to perception between front and back regions, or between the present and the past. It names a structural shift authorizing the tourist to believe she can peer into everything" (*The Tourist* 18). This pretense of barrier removal reoccurs throughout Egan's fiction. To return to Boorstin, he describes how pseudo-events lead to further pseudo-events that purport to explain the previous staged happening; it is in this sense that staged authenticity is a form of infinite regress. As already mentioned, Egan suggests in one article in which she references Boorstin, "the great irony of our technological age is that the phoniness of mediated experience leaves us craving authenticity that only more media can seem to satisfy" ("The 60s" 637). Egan's focus is on tracing how these pseudo-events are constructed and staged, and then how further iterations of such experiences are devised as a reaction to the previous event.

Egan's concern with staged authenticity can be said to gradually shift from the focus on the figure of the tourist to a broader concern with the effects of digital technology on contemporary life. This chimes with MacCannell's suggestion that "a Globally integrated system of values, protocols, and practices did not originate with the internet. It originated in response to the movements, motives, and needs of tourists and was largely realized by the midpoint of the twentieth century" (*The Tourist* xxiii). The "image culture" that Egan explores throughout her career—which she defines as the world of "advertising, fashion, movies, [and] TV . . . that forever slips out of range just at the moment when we feel we've reached it" (Wexler 195)—is one that begins with the vast expansion of tourism, and then moves online. Indeed, Thomas Keene in *Look at Me* makes this connection explicit: "I think the golden age of tourism is basically over, especially for Americans" (261). Thomas argues that his online platform, Ordinary People, which ostensibly provides unfiltered online access to the lives of people across the globe, is an instance of "thinking ahead" and preparing for the shift from physical tourism to digital tourism (261). In Egan's fiction and nonfiction, digital life becomes a vector for staged authenticity, as in her explorations of online dating in her article "Love in the Time of No Time" (2003), Thomas's online platform in *Look at Me,* or the staged authenticity of digital communication in *The Keep*. In this novel, Howard, the hotel manager, lambasts his cousin about the staged authenticity of mobile phone technology: "Who are you talking to on your cell phone? In the end you have no fucking idea" (137). MacCannell's concept is also a means by which to interpret the scenes of punk music in *Goon Squad,* and, as mentioned, Scotty's final performance is a literal image of staged authenticity.

Finally, Egan has a curious relationship to genre. She has written three works that can be described as genre fiction—the aforementioned Gothic novel *The Keep,* the historical novel *Manhattan Beach,* and the thriller "Black Box" (2012), which was published on Twitter—and *Goon Squad* is also an experiment in forms, modes, genres, and perspectives. Egan's relationship with genre connects her to contemporaries such as Michael Chabon, Colson Whitehead, Jonathan Lethem, and many others, a trend I have described elsewhere as the "genrefication" of contemporary American fiction (Moran). It is important to note that this contemporary relationship with genre is distinct from how postmodern writers like Thomas Pynchon or Robert Coover worked with genre. As Andrew Hoberek suggests, "there is a difference between the transitional but still self-consciously 'literary' appropriation of popular genres in the work of authors like Barth and Pynchon . . . and a newer tendency to confer literary status on popular genres themselves" ("After Postmodernism" 238). Jeffrey Williams elaborates further on this generational shift: "The use of popular genres differs from that of the postmodernists, who might have stitched in a vignette featuring Mickey Mouse, for instance, as part of the action, but as parody or farce, for shock or humor" ("Jones" 112). Heather Dubrow proposes approaching works of genre, and genres themselves, through the metaphor of "the color spectrum: no one genre, no one hue appears in isolation, and none appears in its purest state" (28). In this sense, Egan is not an example of the strongest hue of the turn to genre (that mantle belongs to Chabon or Lethem). What is important here is how Egan uses genre, and for what purpose. Egan stated to Zara Dinnen that fiction writers are "creating a simulacrum of the mind-blowing complexity of human experience filtered through perception" ("Artificial"). Genres, and specifically the popular forms that Egan works with, are, in short, another form of staged authenticity, of exploring how experience is managed and filtered. I use the notion of staged authenticity throughout *Understanding Jennifer Egan* to capture the key themes of her fiction: namely, the effects of technological change on contemporary America, the enduring appeal and implications of mediated authenticity, and important role of genres in shaping how fiction is understood.

Biography

Although Egan claims that she finds her own life "boring" as a topic for fiction, elements of her biography do make their way into her writing. Born in Chicago on September 7, 1962, Egan is the child of' parents who divorced when she was seven, and she grew up with her mother and stepfather in San Francisco. She has said, "I feel like I'm from both places" (Tillotson). Egan can be defined as a bicoastal writer, with her texts being largely set in San Francisco or New York, her home since her early twenties. She has often noted that all her fiction begins with "place: a sense of an atmosphere, a location" (Egan and Saunders). She grew up in San Francisco in the aftermath of the 1960s counterculture, and admits to experimenting with "pot, acid, mushrooms, [and] Quaaludes" from a young age ("Patti" 104). Many of these experiences make their way into stories in *Emerald City, The Invisible Circus,* and *A Visit from the Goon Squad.* As a teenager she set her sights on becoming an archaeologist, and she chose the University of Pennsylvania for their well-regarded archaeology program. In September 1980, during her year off before she went to college, she went on her first dig, in Kampsville, Illinois, but, "by day three, I'd renounced my goal of becoming an archeologist," so miserable was the laborious experience of digging ("Archeology"). Using funds she generated working at a Haight Street café, in the summer of 1981 Egan traveled through Europe. She hoped that through a Eurail pass and constant movement she could "cure my absurd lack of worldliness in one grand voyage" ("Keepsake" 196). However, although she experienced panic attacks and went home earlier than planned, this trip cemented what she wanted to do with her life: "it was during that short time in Europe that I decided to become a writer" ("Keepsake" 196). As a result, when she did begin college after this trip, rather than archaeology, she chose English as her major.

Egan began college in the fall of 1981. While at college Egan briefly worked as a model, an experience that she draws upon in *Emerald City* and *Look at Me*. Her preoccupation with surfaces and depths, and the centrality of image culture throughout her writing, can be partly traced to this early experience ("James is a Girl"). At college she edited the university's literary magazine and newspaper, and one of the stories she wrote for her creative thesis, "Letter to Josephine," appears in her debut collection *Emerald City*.[3] It was as an undergraduate at the University of Pennsylvania that she dated Steve Jobs for about a year. This relationship is detailed in Walter Isaacson's fawning biography of Jobs, who tells the story of Egan's mother's shocked dinner guests when, in January 1984, "Steve Jobs—suddenly very famous—appeared at the door carrying a freshly boxed Macintosh and proceeded to Egan's bedroom to set it up" (263). At college Egan read a lot of theory, and Nicholas Dames has noticed the effect of theory on *Goon Squad* in particular. He includes Egan alongside Lorrie Moore, Jeffrey Eugenides, Jonathan Franzen, Sam Lipsyte, Teju Cole, and Ben Lerner as part of the "Theory Generation," referring to the generation of writers who went to university at the high point of theory. Indeed, Martin Paul Eve has traced the constant appearance of academics across her oeuvre ("Structural"). Moreover, she has declared that as a student she found "the practice of literary analysis and argument every bit as urgent and creative an enterprise as writing fiction" ("Notes" 416). After completing her undergraduate studies, Egan received a scholarship to read English at St. John's College, Cambridge. It was here that she met her future husband, David Herskovits (now a well-regarded theater director). At Cambridge she was delighted to begin reading literature rather than to "read about reading instead of reading," as she had back in Pennsylvania (von Arbin Ahlander). While in England Egan wrote a bloated, "monstrous" 600-page manuscript of a novel called *Inland Souls*, and a complete rewrite of this text was to become *The Invisible Circus* (Kois). In 1986, she again decided to travel, this time to China ("Hard Seat"). Egan draws on these experiences in two stories set in China that appear in *Emerald City*—"Why China?" and "After the Revolution." Although Egan is a writer defined by where she has lived—New York, San Francisco, and Chicago—her travel experiences inspire the international settings of her early short fiction in particular.

In 1987, aged 24, Egan moved to New York. She applied to the MFA program at Columbia but was rejected (von Arbin Ahlander). As she states to Dinnen: "I didn't come through the system and I don't teach in the system, so I'm an outsider really" ("Artificial").[4] Postwar fiction has been named "the Program Era" by Mark McGurl, and with good reason, with contemporary publishing symbiotically bound up with numerous university writing programs. Many of Egan's peers followed the path from an MFA to a writing career, such as Michael Chabon (University of California, Irvine), David Foster Wallace (University of Arizona), Junot Diaz (Cornell), Lauren Groff (University of Wisconsin–Madison), and many more. But Egan was not without guidance or support: "I created an ad-hoc MFA by taking workshops people were teaching out of their living rooms in New York when I first got there. Every workshop I sat in gave me something really vital" (Dinnen "Artificial"). She particularly lauds the influence of Philip Schultz—whom she met while working the slush pile for *The Paris Review*—in helping her to develop her voice (von Arbin Ahlander). Egan was not outside the creative writing system, but beside it; it was in this context that she wrote the stories that form *Emerald City,* which is why many of them contain the particular stamp of epiphanic structures promoted by creative writing classes.

Egan supported her writing by working as the private secretary for the Countess of Romanones. As well as being a rich resource for the character of the Countess in *The Keep,* the job's hours, 1:00 PM to 6:00 PM, gave Egan time to hone her craft ("Countess"). She worked for the countess from 1988 to 1990, until a National Endowment for the Arts grant allowed her to pursue writing full-time. While working as a secretary, Egan sold her first stories: "One Piece" to *The North American Review* in 1988, and "The Stylist" to the *New Yorker* in the same year.[5] Once the NEA grant ran out, Egan was still working on her manuscript for what would become *The Invisible Circus.* She found a job at the Tribeca Film Center and began coordinating the First Look Film Series (von Arbin Ahlander). Egan sold her manuscript for *The Invisible Circus* in late 1992 to Nan A. Talese at Doubleday, and the novel was published on December 1, 1994 (Schwartz). Her first story collection was published by Picador in the UK in 1993, but it would not be published in the US until 1996. Following the moderate success of this early collection and her first novel, Egan was offered the chance to begin writing for the *New York Times Magazine,* and on February 4, 1996, "James is a Girl," an exploration of the modeling world, was published, and the research for it formed part of the background for *Look at Me.*

After this initial article, Egan began to write an annual longform piece for the magazine. In 1997, she published her first book review for the *New York Times,* of Aljean Harmetz's *Off the Face of the Earth,* and she has been a generous reviewer of her contemporaries' work ever since. Indeed, part of her regret at the interpretation of her comments on chick lit as a slight is that she is very aware of her own cultural capital: "I blurb a lot of books by women and I'm eager to provide encouragement and support for young women" (Kachka). Throughout *Understanding Jennifer Egan,* I highlight the important role these reviews and nonfiction pieces have played in the development of her fiction.

In 1999, Egan published "Forty-Minute Lunch" in *Harper's,* which was to become the Jules Jones chapter of *Goon Squad* eleven years later. In 2001, a forgettable film adaptation of *The Invisible Circus* was released, of which Egan has said little other than that she was well paid for it and got to meet Cameron Diaz (Hogan). On September 18, 2001, *Look at Me* was published with glowing reviews, although it was obviously a difficult time to publish due to the events of 9/11 a week before. Not only did book sales slump, but the topic of the book, featuring a potential terrorist, made for uncomfortable reading at this time. After *Look at Me,* Egan kept up her yearly works of nonfiction, and then her Gothic thriller, *The Keep,* was published in 2006. That same year, "Selling the General," another future chapter of *Goon Squad,* was published in the oddly titled collection *This is Not Chick Lit: Original Stories by America's Best Women Writers* (which suggests that Egan perhaps did at one point separate her writing from chick lit, a view that she has now changed). The Pulitzer Prize–winning *Goon Squad* was published in 2010, and this led to what she has called a "quantum leap" into a new realm of critical and academic recognition (Cooke). In 2014, Birkbeck held a conference, "The Invisible Circus," which Egan attended, the only conference so far dedicated to her work. After *Goon Squad,* her nonfiction output slowed down a bit. Then, in 2017, *Manhattan Beach* hit the shelves to huge fanfare. Egan's endeavors were also recognized by her peers as she became president of PEN America on March 1, 2018. Throughout this long and winding career path, Egan has, until quite recently, not received the academic attention her work merits. In 2019, *PMLA* dedicated an entire issue to *Manhattan Beach,* but Egan's fiction has yet to be reevaluated and situated within the broader picture of American fiction. *Understanding Jennifer Egan* provides this context, shifting the debate around not only Egan's work but contemporary fiction more broadly.

Chapter Summary

As mentioned, *Emerald City* has a strange publication history. Chapter 2 builds from Martin Paul Eve's exhaustive and granular analysis of the changes and reordering found between the different versions of *Emerald City,* and I offer some possible reasons as to why such changes were made. My main contention in this introductory chapter, however, is that the collection contains, in nascent form, many of the themes and images I trace throughout *Understanding Jennifer Egan.* Far from an instance of juvenilia, these stories are early statements of intent. Comprised of works from Egan's college years in the early 1980s through as late as 1993, *Emerald City* is fascinating for containing many of Egan's signature themes and motifs, such as doubles, twins, and doppelgangers, and teenagers coming of age. It also points ahead to Egan's restless inventiveness of voice, style, and form that defines her later fiction. Moreover, by virtue of being dominated by tourists who never quite find what they are looking for, *Emerald City* serves as an introduction to the concept of staged authenticity.

The third chapter discusses her first novel, *The Invisible Circus.* Although criticism of this work is largely nonexistent, this does not mean it is analytically uninteresting. In fact, the novel clearly presages many of the developments seen in historical fiction in the early twenty-first century, particularly in its focus on the 1970s. I argue that *The Invisible Circus* represents a version of Linda Hutcheon's concept of historiographic metafiction, and by exploring the way 1960s activism led to violent acts of terrorism, Egan depicts the complex relationship between mass media and the countercultural movement. Also, through the tourist experiences of her protagonist, Phoebe, as well as Phoebe's attempts to rekindle the 1960s, Egan further explores images of staged authenticity.

Look at Me is the focus of the fourth chapter, which begins by discussing Egan's strangely underacknowledged and still uncollected journalism, which began in 1996 and continues to this day. The longform pieces she wrote during the years 1996–2000 are a huge influence on *Look at Me,* which in its scope and vision should be thought of as Egan's breakthrough novel. It is a Lynchian text about Charlotte Swenson, a middling fashion model in New York whose face has been reconstructed after a horrific car crash, and Charlotte Hauser, a nondescript teenage girl from Rockford, Illinois. This chapter explores how the model Charlotte's attempts to rebuild her career reveal the role of image culture in defining self-perception. It also analyzes the startlingly prescient image of Z, a Lebanese terrorist adjusting to life in the United States. The chapter concludes with a discussion of Shoshana Zuboff's concept of "surveillance capitalism," arguing that with *Look at Me* Egan examines the rise of surveillance technologies as another form of staged authenticity.

The chapter on *The Keep* first discusses how Egan builds upon the Gothic tradition, and I then explain how she uses the tools of the Gothic to explore the staged authenticity of digital communication. In doing so, *The Keep* becomes a novel of the fantastic, a subgenre of the Gothic defined by structuralist critic

Tzvetan Todorov. A key feature of the fantastic is epistemological and ontological hesitation, for both characters and readers. In *The Keep,* there are hesitations in the formal, staccato way the prose is written, as well as hesitations regarding whether any of the supposedly supernatural events depicted actually take place. I conclude the chapter with a discussion of the redemptive nature of the hotel that Howard builds for Holly, the narrator in the final section of the novel.

The longest chapter explores Egan's most popular and studied piece of fiction to date, *A Visit from the Goon Squad.* As well as tracing its long genesis—as mentioned, one chapter was published in 1998—I explore the unusual mix of influences on the text, and I provide a table to untangle its jumbled timeline. I argue that *Goon Squad* is a summary of all Egan's preoccupations from her earlier fiction: tourism, technology, and time. I finish this chapter by situating her Twitter story, "Black Box," as the hidden track of *Goon Squad,* and argue that it should be considered as a continuation of this text. I then explain the ways in which the 2030s setting of "Black Box"—in which one character from *Goon Squad* is now a cyborg spy—enables Egan to present a particularly dystopian image of where surveillance capitalism could be heading.

In the final chapter on *Manhattan Beach,* I explain Egan's exhaustive research into World War Two, as well as the many literary models she used to help her construct the text. The first of her novels to be set before her own lifetime, Egan's concerns with technology and image culture are largely absent, although I do note the traces of these themes sprinkled throughout the text. *Manhattan Beach* also further confirms how she can be considered as a New York writer, and specifically one of many who have made Brooklyn their home. Contrary to readings of *Manhattan Beach* as a failed example of historical fiction, I argue that it is in fact a pastiche. Following the definitions of Richard Dyer, I explain the distinctions between historical fiction and Egan's use of pastiche, and explore what it means to write a pastiche of this historical period, when America was experiencing so much cultural change in relation to gender, race, and class. I conclude by arguing that while the Second World War may have led to the beginning of the American Century, Egan suggests that the end of this period may soon be coming.

Although I draw connections among Egan's texts throughout this book, each chapter also functions as a standalone investigation. Hence each chapter includes a plot summary to help readers navigate Egan's often complex plotlines, as well as an account of the most important influences on the text under consideration. The purpose of this volume is also to stimulate further discussions of all her texts, which, as mentioned, remain critically understudied.

2

Emerald City

Emerald City first appeared in the UK in 1993 after Egan won the 1992 *Cosmopolitan*/Perrier Short Story Award, but it was not published in the United States for another three years. This delayed publication misled some reviewers of the American edition; Jodee Stanley, for instance, compared it to Egan's 1994 debut novel, *The Invisible Circus,* praising the collection as "reach[ing] beyond her first book, giving us stories that don't simply ring with truth, but shimmer with it" (205). Stanley gets not only the chronology of these texts' initial publication backwards, but also the direction of influence; Egan's early stories in fact point ahead to many of the themes and concepts she will explore over the course of her career, such as coming of age, modeling, and tourism. Moreover, in *Emerald City* Egan constantly switches between perspectives, tenses, and timeframes, a sign of the experimentation that will come to define her fiction. These stories are perhaps most interesting for how they contain, in nascent form, many of the ideas that continue to dominate her work. That said, they also focus on themes and topics that Egan does not return to in her longer fiction. For instance, *Emerald City* features numerous characters who are dealing with the aftermath of financial crimes or mismanagement. The collection also contrasts with her later fiction in that many of its characters are explicitly not interested in or aligned with the protest movements of the 1960s and 1970s, a world that dominates her debut novel, *The Invisible Circus.* For example, in "Passing the Hat," the narrator says, "While the other people our age were protesting the Vietnam War and experimenting with communes, we were buying and redecorating vast houses, overextending ourselves on private schools, and throwing summertime parties in Belvedere and Tiburon" (100). I also note the moments in this collection that reflect Egan's relationship to the literary world of the late 1980s, the time period in which nearly all of these stories were written. So, although these stories lay the thematic groundwork I explore throughout her later fiction, they also are worthy of study in their own right.

The name of the collection is a reference to Frank Baum's *The Wizard of Oz* (1900). Egan notes that this is a metaphor that "fascinates" her, as it refers to "the place you can't reach because it has to glitter at some distance" (Fradkin). In the collection's title story, the protagonist, Rory, uses almost identical language to describe New York: "And it struck him that this was New York: A place that glittered from a distance even when you reached it" (52). This concern with an impossible quest is a central precept in much of her subsequent work; for example, it informs Phoebe's search for the real sixties counterculture in *The Invisible Circus,* and it return in various characters' desire for an authentic self-image in *Look at Me*. In a glowing, perceptive review of the earlier UK version, Clare Messud writes, "The stories in Jennifer Egan's accomplished first collection . . . are about characters, at home and abroad, confronting their own 'tourist-ness': they are people who travel or dream of travelling as a way of affirming themselves, as a way of escaping, or, for those most tourist-like, as an act undertaken in spite of themselves" (24). Messud highlights both the number of tourists in this collection and the dislocation these characters feel from their experiences. Similarly, Stanley states in her review that "Egan writes with glorious clarity about people seeking to transcend their present situations; in the end, however, they tend to arrive at places that are more imagined than real, their longing revealed as naïveté or nostalgia" ("Emerald City"). These readings are suggestive of my focus on Dean MacCannell's concept of staged authenticity, as many characters in this collection find that what they are seeking is always beyond them somehow, like the Emerald City in Baum's world of Oz.

In the only critical article to date on this collection, Martin Paul Eve explores how Egan used the later edition as an opportunity to make some substantive changes to the content and style of many of the stories. Eve analyzes the doubled publication of *Emerald City,* naming these texts "coarchival spaces" that enable critics to see how Egan revised the later version ("Textual" 27). He painstakingly compares the revisions to "The Stylist" and "Sacred Heart" line by line, tracking the differences among the three versions of each story that exist, beginning with their earliest iterations in journals and magazines. He then considers the differences between what he calls Emerald A (the UK version) and Emerald B (the US version). Most strikingly, in addition to sequencing the 1996 version differently, Egan drops the story "After the Revolution" and adds "Why China?" and "Sisters of the Moon." In this chapter, I analyze each story in the collection while building on Eve's scholarship to investigate some of the substantive changes between the two editions.

The stories in *Emerald City* are strewn across the globe, and many of these settings consistently reappear in Egan's writing—San Francisco, New York, Chicago, and Kenya. Similarly, "Sisters of the Moon," as well as being perhaps the most autobiographical work in the collection, explores the 1970s in a similar way as *The Invisible Circus* and *A Visit from the Goon Squad*. Both "The Stylist" and "Emerald City" center on modeling, a topic she returns to in her 1996 article "James is a Girl" and in *Look at Me*. Her constant preoccupation with time is found in "The Watch Trick," and the instruments used to measure time are a recurring motif throughout her fiction. The Gothic trope of twins appears in this collection for the first time in "One Piece," and she has yet to write a novel that does not incorporate twins or doubling in some way. "Puerto Vallarta" and "Sacred Heart" feature both absent and lying fathers, fluid sexual identities, and young women coming of age, topics Egan returns to in *The Invisible Circus, Look at Me, Goon Squad,* and *Manhattan Beach*. There are also biographical connections to Egan's experiences as a child of divorce, and her own global travels are integral to understanding the settings of both this collection and *The Invisible Circus*. After using the contrasting stories set in China from each edition as a springboard to introduce staged authenticity and many of the themes of the collection, I discuss the rest of the stories in order as they appear in the later, US edition, as this structure builds toward the themes that continue into *The Invisible Circus*.

The China Stories

When she was 24 years old Egan traveled through China alone, and she draws on her experience of doing so in both "After the Revolution" and "Why China?" ("Hard Seat"). While reusing the settings and some of the imagery—the "sour smell of China" is mentioned in both—the stories are very different (5; 143). "Why China?" is told from the perspective of a bond trader, Sam, who has been conned out of $25,000 in San Francisco. Unable to let it go, he fudges the numbers at his firm, and is now under investigation. In response, he runs away to China with his wife, Caroline, and their two daughters, Kylie and Jessica. Sam eventually confesses to Caroline that he did in fact steal the money and that he will be found guilty. The story is notable not only for being one of Egan's personal favorites, but because it points ahead to so many of the topics of her later fiction, such as the relationship between art and commerce, characters who are haunted by their past, and how tourists often experience moments of staged authenticity.

San Francisco is a near constant in Egan's fiction, whether as a setting or a place that characters desire to visit, and it is where the family home is in this story. The wife and husband also reminisce about their experiences in Kenya in the Peace Corps, and Kenya reappears in both "The Stylist" and as the location of the "Safari" chapter of *Goon Squad*. In addition to these geographical correspondences, Caroline's career as a sculptor also establishes Egan's preoccupation with the relationship between art and commerce. Supported by her husband's bond trading, Caroline is now so successful that everything she has "yet to sculpt for the next three years was already sold" (8). This connection between financial stability and artistic endeavor constantly reappears throughout the collection and Egan's later fiction, such as the way Howard's financial wizardry enables him to build his dream hotel in *The Keep,* or in the compromises musicians make to succeed in *Goon Squad*. This is reminiscent of what Rachel Greenwald Smith calls a "compromise aesthetic" ("Six Propositions"), whereby artistic choices are often decided by capital—they are, in short, compromised. I discuss this further in Chapter 5, but "Why China?" is the first appearance of the way Egan's fiction often thematizes art's relationship to the market. In a 2011 interview, she acknowledged the role of marketing in her own artistic career: "I'm certainly not against marketing. This is the world we live in, we have to do it" (Kachka). Michael Szalay contends that the entirety of *Goon Squad* is really about marketing (269), and indeed the management and staging of products is a central concern of Egan's fiction. "Why China?" is the first depiction of this tension between authentic artistic expression and the need to market and stage art for it to be discovered, a topic which she explores throughout her career.

Sam is particularly involved in "Brady bonds," a type of restructured bank loan given to poorer countries, as well as investments in "emerging markets" (11). That Caroline's sculpting career is built on the back of these ethically questionable activities suggests that any pretense that her art is authentically separate from the market is a stage that hides an unsavory funding source. Sam is troubled by what he does for a living throughout the story. He finds himself haunted by the Maasai children he worked with in Kenya and is "enraged" when comparing their struggles to the privileges he has purchased for his daughters (6). Throughout Egan's writing there is a preoccupation with characters making compromises in their careers, and in particular how these compromises relate to their academic aspirations. For instance, Sam originally planned to make money and then return to studying anthropology or social work. Eve traces these depictions throughout Egan's later work but does not quite account for the appearance of academic labor in "Why China?" and, as will be discussed later in the chapter, in "Letter to Josephine" (Eve "Structural"). In these early stories, academia is shown to be deeply connected to market forces, as Sam cannot quit to pursue the career he wants because their "overhead was so high" (8); he has compromised for financial gain, and he feels inauthentic to himself as a result.

The narrative begins with the family struggling to get a train to Chengdu, having already traveled from Hong Kong, to Canton, to Kunming. They then continue traveling to Xi'an, and in an amazing coincidence (Egan's fiction is full of these), Sam sees the man who conned him, and who now helps him buy the train tickets to Chengdu. This scene is partly based on Egan's own experiences of how she and her travel partner "had to ask someone at our hotel to write 'Kunming' in Chinese on a slip of paper" ("Hard Seat"). What is notable is who helps them acquire the tickets; the conman, Stuart, buys them and then travels with the family as a guide. Here, Egan connects the idea of a con, or pretense, with being a tourist, so that travel is explicitly connected to being duped or misled. This is ironic considering Sam longs to get away from the staged authenticity of his Kunming environment, where there are Midwesterners at the hotels, and the Chinese people take classes in how to look and act Western (9–10). As MacCannell notes, "Tourists make brave sorties out from their hotels, hoping, perhaps, for an authentic experience, but their paths can be traced in advance over small increments of what is for them increasingly *apparent* authenticity proffered by tourist settings" (*The Tourist* 106). As it becomes increasingly clear that much of what he experiences in Kunming is staged, Sam takes his family to Xi'an, hoping to bump into Stuart. Miraculously, he does so again, and Stuart offers to take Sam to see Buddhist cave paintings, found in an unnamed town outside Xi'an. Sam is compelled to go; like those in *The Wizard of Oz* looking for the Emerald City, Sam hopes that they can access some greater authenticity, some "true" China. Egan herself traveled to Xi'an, but notes some people went much further: "the hard-core travellers were sneaking from Chengdu into Tibet" ("Hard Seat"). Sam goes to Xi'an as he wishes, like these "hard-core travelers" who went to Tibet, to have what he believes will be an authentic cultural experience.

In the unnamed town, the American family becomes an object of intrigue to the locals: "The other diners ceased eating and gathered around to more fully enjoy the spectacle of our presence" (18), and they walk around "trailed by a small crowd of spectators" (19). The acts of looking and being viewed are central to much of Egan's fiction, most obviously in *Look at Me*. Sam has taken his family away from the ogling crowds, and into places where they are the oddity, the attraction for others to see. What MacCannell terms "the dialectic of authenticity" is at work here: "When something is doubled, there is always the question of which side is the true or original side, or the authentic representation" (*The Tourist* 179). The reversal of the viewing relationship here raises the question of where authenticity actually lies, and in turn exposes how Sam's desire for something "real" is indicative of his particular and privileged circumstances. The story ends with his confession to Caroline that he did steal the money, and that Stuart was the man who robbed him.

Published in the *New Virginia Review* in 1990, "After the Revolution" does not appear in the later version of *Emerald City,* and this is perhaps because the ground it treads is covered by other stories. "Why China?" uses the location, while the plot of the traveling divorcee, Katherine Petrie, who foregoes "luxuries one by one," is largely the plotline of "Spanish Winter" (140). Eve reads the title of this story as referring to Katherine's feeling that she came after the revolution, noting that a feeling of having missed the moment points ahead to the themes of *The Invisible Circus* ("Textual" 31). Here, Eve slightly misses the point of the story, which is really a crass analogy between Katherine's divorce and the idea of revolution. "After the Revolution" is about someone outside of the protest movements, which, as will be discussed throughout this chapter, is the focus of many of the stories in this collection. Indeed, a more apt comparison between this story and *The Invisible Circus* is that if Egan's first novel explores America and Europe after the failed revolution of the countercultural movements of the 1960s, *Emerald City* largely focuses on characters who are completely separate from this radical era. MacCannell says that the original plan for *The Tourist,* his landmark 1976 work that investigates the tourist experience as paradigmatic of modern life, was to study revolution and tourism together, and that both represent "a willingness to accept, even venerate, things as they are on the one hand, [and] a desire to transform things on the other" (*The Tourist* 3). Throughout her travels, Katherine venerates China's past as a means to understand the changes in her own life. She sees her trip and her decision to live frugally as her "penance," and hopes that "her reward for these months of exile will be to have all of it back—her husband, her life—restored to her exactly as it was" (149). Her stated desire to live before the revolution does not reflect her regret that she missed seeing the regality of imperial China, but rather that she wants her own life to be back to how it was before her own revolution, before her husband left her and she went to China. She is sleeping with Peter, an older man she does not like much, and is experiencing an unexplainable pain in her side. While out walking in Xi'an, Katherine mysteriously collapses, and Peter carries her all the way back to their hotel so she can get help. The pain subsides once she is back among her creature comforts at the Golden Blossom Hotel, and she realizes that "she has always hated changes—a New Year, birthdays, even shifts in season caused her to cling to what is passing, to cherish it suddenly" (150), but she has no control over her divorce: "Katherine knows, simply, that her life will not be what she has always imagined" (150). Across these two stories set in China, then, one can see Egan's early concerns with staged authenticity and how it relates to travel.

Authenticity in *Emerald City*

"Sacred Heart" is a coming-of-age story about Sarah, who is "almost 15 years old" (39). Eve notes that "Sacred Heart" has 195 edits from the first edition, and although these are mainly corrected typos, there are some substantive changes to central parts of the story ("Textual" 35). Eve establishes that "there is little to no influential path between Emerald A and Emerald B in the editing of 'Sacred Heart,' as the later version is based on edits made to the 1991 *New England Review* edition, rather than the 1993 reissue" (35). Partly inspired by a friend in college who self-harmed, "Sacred Heart" is also influenced by Egan's later article about self-harming teenagers, "The Thin Red Line" (1997). Egan herself notes the "strange symbiosis" (Vida) between her fiction and her journalism, which is visible here; the earlier version led to the assignment, which then led to some of the edits to the 1996 edition of "Sacred Heart."

Set in a Catholic school, the story features a protagonist, Sarah, looking back on a formative episode in her life. It is one of the few stories to be written in the past tense in the entire collection. A new girl, Amanda, asks Sarah to help her cut her arm. Sarah hesitates, but using her own pin, she cuts a bloody A into Amanda's arm, a clear reference to Nathaniel Hawthorne's *The Scarlet Letter* (1850). Following this, Amanda kisses her, which confuses and enraptures Sarah. After a few weeks obsessing over Amanda's every move, Sarah is crestfallen when Amanda runs away from home with her brother. Disconsolate, Sarah decides to cut herself with a razor. Accidentally cutting herself more deeply than she had intended, she is rushed to hospital by her stepdad, Julius, a furrier who she resents having to live with. To staunch the bleeding, Julius uses a fox fur coat he has given to Sarah, which is then ruined by her blood. At the end of the story, Sarah has stopped loathing Julius, and sees Amanda again at a shoe shop, and she is no longer enamored with her.

With the mixture of blood, fur, and sexual attraction, Egan's story serves as a clear allegory for sexual development. Moreover, Sarah finds her parents' sexuality threatening, a refrain which reappears throughout the collection. As mentioned, Julius is a furrier, and so his profession is managing fur and hair; Sarah's resistance to him can therefore be seen as a rejection of puberty. She refuses to wear the coat Julius has gifted her, even after her mother has asked her to. She is particularly troubled that Julius now shares a bed with her mother: "It still amazed me to think that she and Julius shared the big bed where she had slept alone so many years," and she confesses that she "imagined an extra room where Julius slept, an inner door outside which he and my mother kissed good night and then did not meet again until morning" (33). That the pin she uses to cut Amanda is a "goat pin," a present from Julius, further suggests that she finds Julius sexually threatening, the goat being a symbol of lust. The goat is also often used in sacrificial ceremonies, so the bloodletting and marking of Amanda also symbolize a sacrifice. In this sense, Sarah wishes that Amanda could bleed in her place, and it is no coincidence that the story begins with Sarah confessing, "in ninth grade I was a great admirer of Jesus Christ" (19). That she is attracted to Amanda and chooses to mark her with this pin is particularly telling, as is the fact that they then share a kiss (which, as Eve notes, is made more explicit in the later version), as this further connects the story with Amanda's sexual maturation ("Textual" 28).

The other present Julius has given Sarah is a fox fur coat. As a result of her self-inflicted wound, she destroys this coat with her blood, again representative of menstruation and sexual maturity. Sarah's acceptance of Julius happens when she no longer sees him only as a sexual threat: "I knew why my mother loved him, then—he was the sort of man who stayed warm when it was cold out, who kept important tickets and slips of paper inside his wallet until you needed them" (37). In the concluding section of the story, Amanda goes to a school dance with a boy, Michael McCarty, and she accepts that she will have her own love life. This story follows an epiphanic structure, where Sarah accepts herself as a sexual being. By the end of the story, she stops resenting her mother and stepfather, and upon seeing Amanda again she no longer lives vicariously through her; the scent she "inhales" is from her own body (39). Sarah's struggle to distinguish herself from Amanda parallels a central theme of *The Invisible Circus,* in which Phoebe sees herself as a mirror image of her sister, Faith. Moreover, "Sacred Heart," alongside many stories in *Emerald City,* contains a topic that reappears in Egan's debut novel: the ways in which divorces and affairs prompt younger characters, predominantly women, to try to understand the fact that their parents are sexual beings, and the impact this understanding has on their own sexual development.

The title story of *Emerald City* was originally published in the now defunct *Mademoiselle* Magazine in December 1990, with the title "Another Pretty Face." The main character, Rory, is a photographer's assistant to Vesuvi, a fashion photographer in New York, so his job is to manage images, a recurring position of Egan's characters throughout her work. Rory has moved to New York from Chicago and worries that he looks like he is from California due to his sandy blond hair; his character therefore embodies all three of the most common settings in Egan's fiction. The original title refers to Rory's girlfriend, an aspiring model named Stacey, who has recently been rejected for a shoot because she is not "ugly" enough to be a model and does not resemble the "gorgeous mythical monsters" who now dominate cover pages; she is, by implication, only another pretty face (42). The story follows Rory and Stacey as they go for a night out in New York, hoping to find "the people who mattered," even though Rory is unsure who these people are: "Occasionally Rory would be stricken with a sense that they had been exactly where he was only moments before, but had just left" (43–44). A sense of just missing out, of being on the edge of what matters, permeates the whole story, and this is the central theme of *The Invisible Circus,* where no one feels that they truly experienced the sixties.

The events of the story are simple enough: Rory and Stacey meet Vesuvi, who is surrounded by models, for drinks. One of the models, Anoushka (spelled Anushka in the 1993 version), begins to query Stacey on where she has traveled to, in an attempt to humiliate her for her lack of worldliness. When Stacey is asked where she has been, she responds, "I have been to New York" (49). Vesuvi finds this earnest response hilarious, and a confused Anoushka is laughed out of the bar, crying, unsure what has happened. Stacey and Rory return to his apartment to find his roommate, Charles, blowtorching a steak for his work as a food stylist. They discuss their future on the balcony, and Stacey states that if modeling does not work out for her, "then I'll see the world some other way" (54). The story is significant not only for being the first time Egan discusses modeling but for the way she describes New York. It is the Emerald City to the Midwesterners Rory and Stacey—he from Chicago, she from Cincinnati—and a city that rarely lives up to their hopes of what it would be: "Rory knew before he came to New York what sort of life he would have. He'd read about it in novels by hip young authors who lived there" (40). Rory's dreams are a response to the novels of the Brat Pack era, such as Jay McInerney's *Bright Lights, Big City* (1984). This story therefore also finds Egan responding to writers slightly older than her, much like her close contemporary, David Foster Wallace. Indeed, in 1993, the story appeared for a second time, retitled "Emerald City," in the collection *Voices of the Xiled* alongside Wallace's story "Girl with Curious Hair"—a story that is in part a parody of Bret Easton Ellis's *Less than Zero* (1985)—and those of twenty-three other peers. Interestingly, Egan added that Rory read about New York "in novels by hip young authors who lived there" to the 1996 version of *Emerald City,* showing that Egan was becoming aware of her place in the literary world. As Michael Wexler and John Hulme posit in their introduction to *Voices of the Xiled*: "A few months ago it became clear to us that we weren't connecting with any of the images that the new, self-appointed 'twentysomething' authorities had been creating" (xii). Like Wexler and Hulme, Egan has her characters let down by the images they were sold. New York is more like the food that Charles, Rory's roommate, styles as a profession: all surface. Rory and Stacey instead see the management process that goes into making New York, like the Elmer's glue that Charles reveals stands in for milk in cereal commercials. On their walk home from the bar, Rory "searched the dark shopfronts for something, some final thing at the core of everything else," as he desperately tries to find the "true" New York; "but he found just his own reflection and Stacey's" (51). That he sees only their reflections points to what he has found in New York: himself and Stacey, the point being he will find nothing more authentic than that.

The next story, also centered on the lives of models, was originally published in the *New Yorker* on March 13, 1989. The publication of "The Stylist" was a moment when Egan felt she had made it, so overwhelmed was she that she had a story published in such an illustrious magazine (Chamberlin). It was also the first story of hers that appeared in print, although it was her second sale (the first, "One Piece," was sold to the *North American Review*). Like Rory in "Emerald City," the main character is someone who manages how models appear, a thirty-six-year-old stylist called Bernadette. The narrative begins in Lamu, Kenya, and Bernadette notes that they spent the previous day in Mombasa. She comforts one of the models, Alice, who is from Rockford, Illinois. Rockford plays a central role in *Look at Me,* and as in that later novel it operates here as a staid contrast to the jet-setting lives of the models and those around them: "Later today they will fly to Nairobi. Tomorrow morning, New York. Two weeks from now she leaves for Argentina" (65). Alice is homesick, and was until quite recently considered a child; when she was originally discovered at the mall, her snapshot was of her on her brother's shoulders, and the narrator tells us that "at this hour, two months ago, she would be kissing her father good night" (58). Egan contrasts the sexualization of these young women with Bernadette, who, at 36, feels old. Her body is described in detail, and implicitly compared with the wafer-thin bodies of the young models. Modeling is shown to be a staged form of womanhood, where every aspect is managed and framed by people like Rory and Bernadette, whose labor is out of frame and never recorded.

The other main focus of the story is when Bernadette and the photographer, Jann, lie in bed after having sex and discuss their globe-hopping lifestyle. Bernadette notes how all the places merge together, and she finds it hard to distinguish between them in her memory, saying to Jann, "everything fades the minute you're somewhere else" (65). Bernadette's travel has rendered the world indistinguishable; indeed, the numerous travelers of *Emerald City* note their experiences of global homogeneity, an idea that returns in "Letter to Josephine." Bernadette says that lying in bed with him reminds her of something, but that she cannot quite work out what: "It must be one of the few things I haven't seen or done" (60), meaning something that does not fit within this amorphous experience of relentless travel. She tells him she used to be married but was quickly divorced as she felt "restless" (63), and her "only regret . . . is that I hardly have any pictures of myself. All I've got is the shots I styled" (64). The idea of being on the edge or periphery of the frame is central to much of Egan's fiction, and Jann resolves to include Bernadette in a photo, together with Alice and himself, at the end of the story. Bernadette experiences a moment of joy, which she can understand only by comparing it to a longing for something that has already happened: "Between them all is a fragile weave of threads, a spider's web. Bernadette longs for this moment as if it had already passed, as if it could have been. Yet here it is" (68). In a life defined by "restless" movement to manage images, Bernadette can understand this moment only as a record, as something that has already happened. The question of how images influence human memory becomes a pertinent theme throughout Egan's subsequent fiction.

The first piece of fiction Egan ever sold, "One Piece," appeared in the *North American Review* in June 1989. Egan regards this story as her breakthrough moment, as it was the first time she was allowed to read a story all the way through in her writing group: "I don't think I've ever felt more of a clear triumph, a sense of finally having crossed over a chasm" ("Jennifer Egan: Writer"). "One Piece" is a partly Gothic coming-of-age story about a young girl, Holly, whose brother, Bradley, accidentally killed their mother in a freak car accident. The girl was too young to remember the accident, being only one at the time (indeed, in the earlier versions, Egan's math is slightly wrong, and Holly's age is too young to have even been born yet).[1] Bradley is a boy with impulse control issues who loves making models, and who unintentionally causes accidents and trouble: he pushes his stepsisters off the tire swing, and concusses Holly with a baseball. During a family holiday at Lake Michigan, Holly is trying to find the "one piece" that will make their model family work, like Bradley's models (82). With Bradley watching her, she dramatically leaps into a bonfire from a tree so Bradley can rescue her and be the hero. The story ends with the family united again, and the staged authenticity of his rescue—planned by Holly—becomes the grounding for a happier future.

Intriguingly, "One Piece" is the story which has been most comprehensively changed in the later editions, as its narration is shifted from past tense to present tense. The ending is changed dramatically as a result; rather than Holly looking back on the incident, it becomes a moment when the young siblings acquire some closure on the death of their mother. There are other details changed, too, such as the models Bradley makes—instead of the *Titanic,* he is instead building *Apollo 13*. Egan has made this change because the theme of the story, the "one piece" that Holly is desperate to find to make their new family model work (82), mirrors what happened to *Apollo 13*—it was just one faulty piece of equipment, the oxygen tank, which led to an emergency landing. *Apollo 13* also better captures the success of Holly's plan, given that the astronauts all returned safely, as the passengers of the *Titanic* obviously did not. "One Piece" is also the first instance of a doubling or twinning in Egan's fiction: Bradley tells Holly that she looks just like their dead mother (76). As mentioned in the introduction, doubling, doppelgangers, and twins appear in all of Egan's work. What is interesting here is that Holly's resemblance to her mother is about perception, or rather Bradley's lack of it: "My skin is darker than hers, and a little shiny. I have freckles on my arms, and when I try to sing, I hit every wrong note" (84). The implication is that Bradley, ravaged by guilt, sees his mother's face everywhere, but Holly's actions save Bradley from feeling eternally at fault. This points ahead to the redemptive function of Howard's hotel in *The Keep,* and the many other images of staged redemption seen throughout her writing.

Published in *GQ* in November 1990, "The Watch Trick" follows ex-Army friends Sonny and James, who are on a boat in Lake Michigan, along with James's wife, Diana, and Sonny's young girlfriend, Billie. Sonny has seduced Billie away from her wedding, and is generally a man of excess, fueled by fast-food industry investments "he'd had the prescience to make early on" (87). This means he does not have to work; once again, Egan depicts capital as transformative and liberating to those who were able to accumulate it. However, just as the fast food that has made him rich cannot satiate, Sonny cannot settle, jumping from partner to partner. On the boat, Billie finds out that Sonny often has these romantic flings, and, as a response to James' goading, Sonny tells James that he and Diana had sex a long time ago. James and Sonny come to blows, and then they head back to shore. The story concludes with Billie returning to her fiancé, and Sonny refusing to give up the lifestyle that is slowly killing him.

Sonny, whose name indicates his lack of maturity, first seduced Billie by throwing an expensive watch into the sea, claiming time stops when he is with her. Stopped clocks are a contrived image of revolution in *The Invisible Circus,* and a broken watch is evidence of Eddie Kerrigan's staged death in *Manhattan Beach*. Time and its measurement are central elements of Egan's Proustian-infused novels— in particular, time is the "goon" of the title in *A Visit from the Goon Squad*—and "The Watch Trick" marks the first instance of time appearing as an explicit concern in her work. Time is also at work in the way Diana compares her appearance to the much younger Billie, thinking that the veins on her legs "seemed more offensive now" (a line added to the 1996 edition), just as Bernadette fears she is aging in "The Stylist" (87). James and Diana, too, look to the past; they already had their "perfect moment" with Sonny in the early

1970s, going from "party to party" (87). Although Sonny has, like the watch he has thrown into the water, refused to change, James has moved on from his college basketball stardom at University of Michigan to work his way up as a corporate lawyer. Diana is just finishing her PhD in film studies, her dissertation being titled "Crisis and Catharsis in the Films of Alfred Hitchcock" (88). Diana's constant viewing of Hitchcock's films has led her to be "weirdly nostalgic as she watched, as if her own life had been like that once—dreamy, Technicolor—but had lost these qualities through some misstep of her own" (88). The Hitchcock references are a bit of a red herring as far as the narrative goes, as the plot is actually reminiscent of Roman Polanski's debut *Knife in the Water* (1962). How art impacts memory is a theme that recurs in each of Egan's novels, particularly characters who are nostalgic for their lives in the seventies. By the end of the story, a year after the disastrous boat trip, Diana has begun teaching at the University of Illinois at Chicago. Once again, academic pursuits are funded by a partner with a more stable career, in this instance by James's law work.

Another story centered on young stockbrokers, set in San Francisco, and looking at the aftershocks of divorce, "Passing the Hat" was first published in *GQ* in April 1991. It is told from the perspective of a woman who moved with her husband, Ted, as part of a migration from "drab, Midwestern towns" to San Francisco, with "all of us making money, having children, and intending to do a great deal more of both" in the early 1970s (100). This is a story that focuses on Nixon's silent majority: "While the other people our age were protesting the Vietnam War and experimenting with communes, we were buying and redecorating vast houses, overextending ourselves on private schools, and throwing summertime parties in Belvedere and Tiburon" (100). Rather than chronicling the protest movements, this a narrative about those who have bought completely into the then emerging world of neoliberal capitalism. The story shifts gears when it is revealed that the narrator is divorced; Ted has left her for a younger woman and had another child. She has found out that Ted also cheated on her with Catherine Black, a socialite who drifted through their group of friends and dated many of the men; Catherine is the "hat" that is passed around and money is placed into. The narrator remembers a skiing trip—again, travel is a big part of this story—where she shared a ski lift with Catherine. She feels she was not party to the realities of what was going on in her social world, and that Catherine was "quietly watching me live" (110). Memory is a central theme of the story and is compared to an investment: "When it comes to memory, I suppose, we're all passing the hat" (102). Here, Egan suggests memory is a collective experience, one that everyone needs to invest in for it to be maintained, a central theme in her first novel, and in *Goon*

Squad. "Passing the Hat" points ahead to her preoccupation with collective memory and the way generations define their experiences by the meaning they invest in each moment.

Published in *Ploughshares* in 1991, "Puerto Vallarta" is set both in Chicago and Puerto Vallarta, Mexico. The narrator, Ellen—a name Egan reuses in *Look at Me,* with Ellen Metcalf the name of the mother of the younger Charlotte—discovers her father has been having an affair. The story begins with a family holiday in Puerto Vallarta, moves back to Chicago, and then returns to Puerto Vallarta. As with "Sacred Heart," part of the coming-of-age aspect of this story is Ellen recognizing the sexual lives of her parents. For instance, before she has discovered the affair, she notices the way her parents look at each other, and "felt a current of something between them that startled her" (113). The affair is discovered when she goes to drink at a Mexican restaurant just outside Chicago (unnamed in the 1993 version, called "Mama Santos" in the later edition), and sees her father, who she had previously believed was on a business trip to Australia, with another woman. Ellen longs to be a child again, before she knew of her father's affair: she "wished she were back at the age when she would howl shamelessly while her mother used a tweezer to pick bits of gravel from her skinned knees" (116). As she witnesses her father leave with the other woman, "it seemed like an ancient memory, a scene from her childhood" (115). For Ellen, this event signals the end of her childhood, another instance of a young person coming of age through recognition of a parent as having a sex life.

When the family return to Puerto Vallarta, Ellen goes with her father to visit his friend, a contractor called Ed Morgan. As in "Why China?" and, as we will see in the next story, "Spanish Winter," characters who have committed financial crimes appear frequently in this collection; Ed is currently hiding from people he has lied to. Ed also gets Ellen drunk, plying her with vodka, behavior that has disturbing overtones as he begins their interaction by saying it is "no wonder" that Ellen's father keeps her hidden, given her alluring appearance (119). Indeed, drunk and confident, Ellen then explores her newfound sexuality, recklessly standing alone in a group of young Mexican men. In an unfortunate example of racist stereotyping, Egan presents these Mexican men as a non-individuated sexual threat to her white female protagonist, the kind of caricature that is absent from her later fiction. As they watch Ellen, she becomes "conscious of her thin, bare arms, the tiny hairs on her thighs" (122). One of the men tries to lead her away, but her father intervenes, and she is saved from what Egan implies would have been a horrible fate. She then reveals her father's affair to her mother, and she walks into the ocean, which purifies the same thighs she was aware of when the men were leering: "Ellen took a few more steps until the churning water scrubbed her shins, then her thighs" (125). Here, Ellen washes away her father's infidelities, and resolves to move on with her mother by her side. "Puerto Vallarta" is thus a notable story in Egan's catalog because of the use of water as a means of cleansing Ellen, and water is a particularly important image throughout her work, particularly the New York waterfronts in *Manhattan Beach*.

Originally published in the Fall 1989 edition of *Ploughshares,* "Spanish Winter" follows the recently divorced Alison (Alexis in the earlier version), who has resolved to rid herself of all worldly possessions. In Spain, she begins her travels in Madrid, then Córdoba, then back north to Toledo, and then south to Granada, where the majority of the story takes place. This haphazard, zigzag journey is representative of her state of mind; all that matters to her is that she is traveling: "I've been an off-season traveler since my divorce, and this winter I'm in Spain" (128). In Granada, she is robbed of her money and passport (which is based on a real experience Egan had while traveling) and then bumps into an old college friend, Jake, who witnesses her getting robbed again but chases the robbers down and retrieves her new purse. Jake invites her to Morocco, and she accepts. Travel is again depicted as an escape, a pause of an actual life, much like in "Why China?" and "After the Revolution": "A last stop, I think, before I go back home to begin again. I'm young, headed to Morocco on vacation. In Morocco it is summertime" (140).

"Spanish Winter" is another story featuring financial crimes. Jake, the college friend she miraculously bumps into, has "lost a lot of people's money" and done a "stupid thing" (137). Americans abroad are always depicted as escaping from something: here, Alison is escaping from her divorce and the limited amount of time she spends with her daughter, Penny (called Alice in the 1993 edition), while Jake is escaping his financial misdemeanors. *Emerald City* is a collection full of characters who are traveling to avoid the consequences of their financial misdeeds. Indeed, in this story Alison is away from Penny, her daughter's name a clear monetary pun. The other notable aspect of "Spanish Winter" is how Alison interacts with her daughter: "I spend these days waiting in cafes, writing postcards to Penny. At home she will attach them to the refrigerator using fruit-shaped magnets. She does this carefully, plotting my journey in perfect sequence. When I return she will narrate it like a story" (133). The staged authenticity of postcards is a central part of travel for Egan; the postcards that Faith sends to Phoebe and her family in *The Invisible Circus,* for example, become the basis for Phoebe's future travels. When she gets to Europe, she finds nothing is quite as Faith described it in her postcards. Similarly, in *Look at Me* Charlotte uses her grandparents' letters to guide her early

New York experiences. This disjuncture between representation and reality is an important image for how travel functions in Egan's fiction to misrepresent, misreport, or distort places and experiences.

Originally written in Egan's college years and published in *Boulevard* in Spring 1990, "Letter to Josephine" features Lucy, a young woman on holiday in Bora Bora, Tahiti, with her immensely wealthy husband, Parker, who runs the family pharmaceutical business. The title of the story refers to a letter that Lucy imagines writing to her childhood friend, Josephine, about her new life of wealth, travel, and privilege, and comparing it to the way they "used to pore over magazines and imagine living other people's lives" (151). She never sends the letter, and instead uses it to consider the life she now has. This story is similar to "The Stylist" in the way that global travel has blurred different locations into one: "They have been all over the world, Lucy thinks. . . . She clings to names, to snapshots and matchbooks, but the many seasons have mingled hopelessly" (145). Again, travel has homogenized the world, and she can only tell apart the locations "according to which bathing suit she was wearing—the polka-dotted one in Cannes, the striped red in Spain. But the sand and water around the bathing suits all look the same" (145). This blurring together of experiences is connected here to power and privilege, rather than being something endemic to everyone in the contemporary world. She does not even know the cost of where she is staying, "because Parker handles that" (141), so she is completely without any point of reference for assessing the value of what she is doing. In Tahiti, Lucy becomes obsessed with a stunningly beautiful woman whom she voyeuristically watches head into her bungalow to have sex. She has an experience of seeing what she believes is a backstage space, an authentic view into someone else's life. She is fulfilling the quest of what MacCannell defines as the motivation of touristic consciousness: "Touristic consciousness is motivated by its desire for authentic experiences" (*The Tourist* 101). Lucy feels she has seen a back region, an authentic experience of someone else's holiday. By the end of the story, she thinks she sees the same woman as a waitress in Santa Barbara, but she cannot be sure: "She tries to remember Bora Bora. Like all their vacations, that one has faded, blurred with other hotels, other beaches" (158). All of her vacations blur into one, and the story concludes with her imagining one last conversation where Josephine tells her, "You're in the perfect spot" (159). As the world blurs into a single experience for Lucy, the implication is that her wealth allows her to exist in one perfect state in which she simply watches others.

"Letter to Josephine" is perhaps most important for the way it depicts academia. Parker quit a PhD at Yale to run his father's business, and so he spends each holiday reading about a war: in Tahiti, it is the Crimean War he is focused on. It is noted that "after a few drinks" he still talks "about the late-night arguments over Macaulay and Gibbon and Michelet" he had in graduate school (148).[2] The reason he quit academia is "obvious": "Parker is a man of creature comforts. He grew up rich, and it is hard to imagine him living any other way" (149). Later in the story, Lucy even directly states to Parker that "the money" is why he quit (156). Here, academia is depicted as a touristic pursuit, for people taking a break. Parker's reluctance to be poor ultimately disqualifies him from academic life, a theme of academic precarity that, as Eve explores, is present in *The Keep* and *Goon Squad* (*Literature* 21).

Egan draws on her life for many of the stories in this collection—travel locations, her experiences as a child of divorce, and many of the stories feature young women coming of age. The most autobiographical story in the collection is "Sisters of the Moon," which was first published in the *New Yorker* in 1993. Tally is the fourteen-year-old narrator living in San Francisco in 1974. Egan has noted that as a teenager, she and two friends had "prolonged nocturnal wandering[s]" around San Francisco ("Patti" 104), and Tally and her two friends, Angel and Liz, do something similar. They walk to Union Square where they hang out with men much older than them, Silas and Irish. Egan has mentioned in many interviews she first dropped acid when she was fourteen, and this is the centerpiece of this story: Tally, fourteen, takes acid, and the friends graffiti the title of the story all over San Francisco. While high, she discusses with Silas how she always feels on the peripheries of San Franciscan life in the mid-1970s: that she watches and does not take part is, as Silas says, "what'll save you," as many of the others will die (169). The story concludes with Silas noting that in twenty years, in 1994, people will be "wishing they'd been here the first time," which has a particular resonance with Egan's first novel, originally published on December 1, 1994, and set in San Francisco in late 1970s. As well as being deeply autobiographical, "Sisters of the Moon" is the text that depicts the aftermath of the 1960s in San Francisco, which is a theme of both *The Invisible Circus* and *Goon Squad*.

Emerald City, then, is a collection that points ahead to many of the settings, themes, and ideas that Egan develops in her later fiction. The way she edited the later version, not only excising stories but making big changes to tenses, phrasing, and character names is a unique way of tracking her development as a writer. In particular, in the edit to "Emerald City" we can see her growing sense of her own place in the literary world in the added reference to the New York writers who made it big in the 1980s, like Ellis, Tama Janowitz, and McInerney. Moreover, Egan has repeatedly claimed she loathes to write about her own life, yet her early writing finds her building from her own experiences of travel and her adolescence in the 1970s. These experiences also form the basis of her first novel, *The Invisible Circus,* which, in contrast to many of the stories in *Emerald City,* focuses exclusively on the events and the aftermath of the protest movements of the 1960s.

3

The Invisible Circus

In the summer of 1981, toward the end of a gap year between high school and college, Egan traveled through Europe. She hoped that with the aid of a Eurail pass and constant movement, she could "cure my absurd lack of worldliness in one grand voyage" ("Keepsake" 196). However, she began to experience panic attacks, and ended up calling her mother from Rome "weeping, and went home early" ("Keepsake" 196). She notes that "it was during that short time in Europe that I decided to become a writer" ("Keepsake" 196). In her travel diary of the time—which she reprints in a later article—she resolved to come to terms with her "vague, shapeless whirlpool of fear that my life has not been 'real'; i.e. has not, and will not" ("Keepsake" 200), by writing about it. That journey across Europe and the feeling of not being "real" were to become central to the plot of *The Invisible Circus.*

But writing the novel was not plain sailing. At twenty-two—four years before her first short story was published—Egan had a "monstrous" 600-page first draft of a novel titled *Inland Souls* she had written when studying at Cambridge (Kois). The title is from Emily Dickinson's poem "Exultation is the Going," and the plot was centered on the aftermath of the 1960s and her travel experiences. She received pretty clear feedback on how awful the text was: "I would send this book to people . . . and they would become unreachable. And that includes my mother" (Kois). After a complete rewrite and a new title, *The Invisible Circus* was published on December 1, 1994. Although Egan downplays the novel as "not a masterpiece, but a start" ("Keepsake" 200), she has nonetheless expressed frustration regarding its reception, and particularly with how reviewers largely ignored its key themes: "I could talk very theoretically about that book, but most people would say, 'What are you talking about? This is a book about two girls and a girl whose older sister has committed suicide'"

(Miller). Although this is broadly the plot, *The Invisible Circus* is better understood as a melodramatic novel about the legacy and valorization of 1960s protest movements. Indeed, Egan says, "For me a story is just not interesting if there isn't a philosophical query along with it," and so this chapter aims to excavate that query (Miller). Set in 1978, the story follows Phoebe O'Connor, an eighteen-year-old who has never really recovered from the suicide of her sister, Faith, which happened on November 21, 1970. Faith was particularly close to their father, a failed painter who worked unhappily at IBM and died of leukemia when the sisters were young. Phoebe travels across Europe, visiting all of the places Faith had been to previously: London, Amsterdam, Reims, Paris, Berlin, and Italy. In Berlin she bumps into Wolf, Faith's boyfriend up until her death. From here they travel together to Corniglia, Italy, as Phoebe wishes to visit the cliff where Faith leapt to her death. On the long drive down, Wolf and Phoebe begin a passionate affair. It is in Corniglia that Wolf tells Phoebe that Faith joined the Red Army Faction, the violent left-wing group made up of student radicals, and after they abandoned her, she joined a similar group called the June Second Movement. As part of this group, she accidentally killed a man with a bomb, and Wolf believes it is her guilt at this action that drove her to jump. Phoebe then returns to San Francisco—the entire trip lasts three months, from July 2 to September 3—to begin her studies at Berkeley, and to move on with her life, having finally laid the ghost of her sister to rest.

The Invisible Circus is a historical novel that queries the authenticity of collective memory. In particular, this novel depicts the transition from protest to violence, from activism to terrorism, as Phoebe's sister, Faith, moves from being a sixties idealist to becoming a member of the Baader-Meinhof group in Berlin. In depicting this transition, Egan develops a partly dismissive concept of the 1960s counterculture as having been blown out of all proportion, and the text often alludes to the childishness of those involved. For instance, the "invisible circus" of the title—a reference to The Diggers—is described by Faith as a "grown-ups' funhouse" (53). Phoebe's experiences are also repeatedly connected to those of Alice in Wonderland, implying a fantastical world she cannot quite reach, much like the Emerald City in Egan's earlier short story (47, 51). Egan explains this transition to violence as one produced by the concomitant rise of the mass media in tandem with the tumultuous events of the 1960s. She has cited the importance of Todd Gitlin's sociological and autobiographical accounts of the era on her depiction of the process, in which he charts the sensational events the mass media sought to cover in this era, and that in response, activists began to create such spectacles (Reilly 455).[1] *The Invisible Circus* is also, as Pankaj Mishra notes, an account of "an American abroad," as we follow Phoebe as she traces Faith's steps across Europe, continuing the theme of travel and escape that was so prominent in *Emerald City* ("Modernity"). Finally, this novel finds Egan beginning to explore the blending of image and reality that she will continue to develop from this novel and throughout her career, as Phoebe understands "the movement" only through images, memories, and hearsay. From the staging of what the 1960s meant to the staging of touristic experiences and then the staged, violent authenticity of terroristic acts, each element of *The Invisible Circus* is infused with staged authenticity.

Authenticity and Historical Fiction

In his canonical formulations of the postmodern era, Fredric Jameson argues that "it is safest to grasp the concept of the postmodern as an attempt to think the present historically in an age that has forgotten how to think historically in the first place" (*Postmodernism* ix). But, even if one accepts that Americans at the end of the twentieth century had forgotten how to think historically, fiction writers in the 1990s were nevertheless desperately trying to do so. John Duvall notes that historical fiction was a preoccupation of many American writers during the 1990s, as is evident in texts such as Norman Mailer's *Harlot's Ghost* (1991), Don DeLillo's *Underworld* (1997), Thomas Pynchon's *Mason & Dixon* (1997), and Toni Morrison's *Paradise* (1997; 126). Egan's debut was therefore part of a reflective moment in American literary history, when the close of the Cold War triggered many writers to look back and consider how the present came to be. Egan's debut novel also fits into a broader reappraisal of the 1970s seen across recent fiction, which Nicholas Dames has named "Seventies Throwback Fiction." Curiously, Dames does not mention Egan at all, even though she explores the 1970s in both *The Invisible Circus* and *Goon Squad*. Indeed, despite almost uniformly positive reviews upon its publication, the broader reappraisal of Egan's work after the success of *Goon Squad,* and the clear thematic connections to the much-studied latter novel, *The Invisible Circus* has been largely ignored in academic criticism.[2] Early reviews focused on the emotional power of the novel rather than its insight into the collective loss of 1960s radicalism. It is indeed a melodramatic, plot-driven bildungsroman about the aftermath of a family tragedy. Moreover, it is partly a romance, and some sex scenes were republished in the collection *The Good Parts: The Best Erotic Writing in Modern Fiction* (2000). These aspects of the plot are emphasized in the 2001 film adaptation, but focusing on these points alone elides how Egan's novel is also an important text in the broader reappraisal of the sixties and seventies seen across contemporary fiction. Mark West situates the novel as one of the earliest examples of "the contemporary sixties novel," which comprises some forty novels from 1995 to 2018 (210).[3] West discusses the novel alongside Dana Spiotta's *Eat the Document* (2006) and

Christopher Sorrentino's *Trance* (2005), the latter of which focuses on Patty Hearst, with whom Phoebe is preoccupied throughout *The Invisible Circus*. He argues that Phoebe has made Faith into a "myth," and it is the construction of this myth that I explore throughout this chapter (214).

The 1990s also witnessed important theoretical debates, particularly between Linda Hutcheon and Jameson, regarding how writers understand and represent history. Jameson contended that "the historical novel can no longer set out to represent the historical past; it can only 'represent' our ideas and stereotypes about that past" (25). *The Invisible Circus* engages with precisely this point in regard to the 1960s. As Phoebe delves into Faith's past, she discovers that no one feels they actually experienced the 1960s in the way it has been represented and mythologized in the decades since, so immortalized has it been in what Gitlin calls "a collage of fragments scooped together as if a whole decade took place in an instant" (*Sixties* 3). But one of Phoebe's discoveries is that the images she has tried to chase are stereotypes, snapshots—many of which are postcards from Faith—which are actually fictions of the era themselves. In this sense, Egan's novel represents a slight twist on Hutcheon's famous theory of "historiographic metafiction," which is defined by "its theoretical self-awareness of history and fiction as human constructs" (*Poetics* 5). Phoebe discovers that her image of what constituted the authentic sixties is something constructed; the "metafiction" in this novel is not the metafictional impulses of Egan, but the self-awareness of the protagonists involved in the protest era. Egan's concern therefore is with the authenticity of these historical events that were, in a sense, manufactured by and for the mass media. As Gitlin argues, "The media had discovered youthful protest, and in the process bent the images to the sensational" (*Sixties* 232). Egan ultimately argues that this focus was bound to end in the most sensational acts possible, namely violent terrorism.

In this sense, Egan partly shares David Foster Wallace's sentiment, written at a similar time, about those protesting the Vietnam War: "They may have hated the war, but they also wanted to be seen protesting on television" (160). However, Egan is much less dismissive of this era than Wallace; Egan gives due credence to the historical weight and import of the events of these years, both for the characters in her novel and in the popular imaginary, while still registering her dissatisfaction with the need to constantly return to them. Throughout *The Invisible Circus*, her focus is on how the historical records that Phoebe follows—Faith's postcards, the old issues of the *Oracle* she spends "hours poring over" (29), and the newspaper cuttings from Faith's noticeboard—are staged snapshots and glimpses of the era. As Phoebe gradually discovers what Faith did in Berlin, she realizes that the story she has told herself about her sister is exactly that—a story. The bildungsroman is complete once Phoebe realizes "she would stand somewhere and look back, she would live a life," rather than keep wearing her sister's ill-fitting clothes and trying to recreate the past (279). As she comes to know the realities of her sister's actions and death, Phoebe's own life comes into sharper focus. Phoebe's journey leads her to discover that the version of the sixties that "had been named and written about" by 1978 is a mythopoetic construction that does not hold up to scrutiny (29). In short, Phoebe has been chasing a staged form of authenticity, an invisible circus she can never quite reach.

The opening lines of the novel relate Phoebe's feeling that she has "missed it," referring to a "Revival of the Moons" festival, an event which intended to recreate a festival held ten years previously in 1968 (3). This is a feeling Egan has noted she felt herself growing up: not having missed the sixties, but having just missed it, as Phoebe just misses this festival (Schwartz). Jeffrey Williams labels this a generational trait, naming Egan's generation "generation Jones," which is "characterized by a yearning (as in 'jonesing'), a feeling that it missed out, arriving after the legendary flourishing of the 1960s" (95). That Phoebe then sees the festival being dismantled indicates how the novel's opening is a metaphor for a broader cultural feeling experienced in the 1970s, of having just missed living through momentous historical events. At the festival, Phoebe bumps into Kyle, who knew Faith, and smokes a joint with him at his Cole Street apartment. Kyle notes that he felt like he "wasn't really there," in regard to the events of the sixties, and Phoebe has to reassure him that he was (11). In the opening scenes of the novel, then, Egan immediately sets up a sense that nobody feels like they have experienced the sixties: Phoebe and her generation feel like they have just missed out on it, and Kyle, who was actively a part of the era, feels like he was not even there. Phoebe's sense of having "missed" everything leads her to feel that "her present life was unreal and without significance" (11). Jameson notes that the 1970s "seemed most of the time to consist in having no specificity, particularly after the uniqueness of the preceding period" (*Postmodernism* 296). Phoebe dances in Faith's room, trying to be her sister, but is "jerked out" of this fantasy by the realization "that her present life was nothing but the aftermath of something vanished" (67). She longs not only to be Faith, but to have been Faith; she licks her palm when it is accidentally covered in Faith's ashes (14), and because she dresses like Faith, people she encounters, such as Kyle and Wolf, note how much she looks like her. Her sense of self is defined by how much she can inhabit Faith's existence, rather than her own. Phoebe's actions are representative of the decade writ large: The 1970s are depicted as an aftermath, as defined by attempts to recover from the previous generation.

Egan also infuses the era with nostalgia, especially in San Francisco. Phoebe works at a coffee shop run by gay men (a job which Egan herself held as a teenager), and she works on Haight Street, a central location of the hippie movement. The Haight Street sign has been stolen so many times by "nostalgics" that Phoebe notes that the city has stopped bothering to replace it (63). In the late 1970s the Haight-Ashbury area is now dominated not by hippies, but by tourists: "traversing Haight Street with maps aloft, aware that they were close, so close, but unable to find the dead center they sought" (63). Like Sam and his family in "Why China?" the tourists that Phoebe sees in San Francisco in 1978 are trying to find an authentic "center" that is always out of grasp. All that remains of the sixties are some tacky commercial enterprises, "whole-food stores with their bins of knobby fruit, head shops, an occult store full of shrunken heads and tinted crystal balls" (63). These are staged scenes of authenticity, designed for tourist consumption. As MacCannell argues, "the creation of staged authentic environments is such a profitable enterprise" precisely because "they seem to resolve everyone's contradictions," such as here allowing for commerce and tourism to flourish in areas that once aimed to reject such a world ("Why" 337). Phoebe also witnesses the darker side of the 1960s, as she regularly gives lemons to young "vagabond kids" who use them to shoot up heroin (65). Egan depicts San Francisco in the late 1970s as, much like Phoebe herself, existing in the shadow of the 1960s.

Phoebe decides to leave this milieu of nostalgia and heads for Europe, determined to trace her sister's journey using the postcards Faith sent her while traveling. She is living out a version of what Jameson terms nostalgia for the present, a feeling Egan locates as common in the 1970s. Wishing to relive the experiences of the 1960s in the late 1970s, Phoebe's present is defined by nostalgia, like the "nostalgics" she derides for stealing the Haight Street road sign. Her trip is in many ways a pilgrimage; as MacCannell notes (via Everett C. Hughes), "The motive behind a pilgrimage is similar to that behind a tour: both are quests for authentic experiences. Pilgrims attempted to visit a place where an event of religious importance actually occurred. Tourists present themselves at places of social, historical, and cultural importance" ("Staged Authenticity" 593). Her journey is a pilgrimage to access some of the authenticity that she feels Faith experienced, and she even has a spiritual guide in the ghostly presence of Faith, as well as the canonical (to Phoebe) texts of Faith's postcards.

But that is not the only reason Phoebe wishes to escape; though she tells her mother she feels like a "zombie" and longs to experience more of the world, the trigger for her leaving is discovering that her mother is dating her longtime boss and film producer, Jack Lamont (61). As with many of the young women in *Emerald City,* her mother's sex life is a shock to her; Kyle laughs at Phoebe's assertion that her mother is "past romance" now she is 47, and she has never considered that her mother could have a "secret life" (74). This shock leads her to feeling betrayed by her mother, with whom she regularly falls asleep watching *The Rockford Files* (the second reference to Rockford, a place central to *Look at Me,* in Egan's fiction after the brief nod to this city in "The Stylist"). Finally, the other reason she can travel is that she can afford to; her father left her five thousand dollars in his will. As often happens in Egan's fiction, money generates much of the plot, from Sam's bond trading in "Why China?" to Anna's savings allowing her to move to San Francisco at the end of *Manhattan Beach*. Here it is the money left by Gene, Phoebe and Faith's father, that enables them both to travel to Europe, ten years apart. It is across Europe that the majority of the novel takes place.

Image and the Real

Upon arriving in London, Phoebe feels she has found what she was looking for; she writes in her notebook, "In England everything is more real. The money is colorful, the coins are heavy like real gold, the parks are greener, the people have beautiful accents. There are terrorists all over, and bomb threats. Nothing is the way I'm used to. This is the real world and I'm totally alive, for the first time ever" (108). The nostalgia for the present that she felt in San Francisco is, initially, satiated by London, which appears to match the image she had of the city. However, after a week in which she has to hastily leave Harrods due to a bomb threat and a kindly stranger explains the motivations of the numerous terrorist groups who could be culpable, the staged authenticity of London begins to obscure her memories of Faith: "She began to fear that her own presence was erasing her sister's, blurring it to vagueness" (111). She scolds herself for not making "some crucial leap," and "she left London determined to push herself harder" (111).[4] Phoebe's hope that at the next place she will discover the ostensibly "real" world she is looking for echoes MacCannell's description of the tourist: "Tourists make brave sorties out from their hotels, hoping, perhaps, for an authentic experience, but their paths can be traced in advance over small increments of what is for them increasingly *apparent* authenticity proffered by tourist settings" (*The Tourist* 101). As with many of the tourists seeking greater authenticity in *Emerald City,* it becomes increasingly apparent that the authenticity she initially felt in London was a stage, and so she leaves in search of a more authentic experience.

After London, Phoebe travels to Amsterdam, where she asks around for anyone who knew Faith. A young man named Nico takes her to Karl, a drug dealer who was around during the late 1960s. Karl not only says that he knew Faith, but suggests that the 1970s are defined by people who went "too far" in the sixties and became "the opposite" (120). Foreshadowing what Phoebe will learn about Faith's actions later in the novel, Karl argues that the violence that Faith found herself involved in was the logical endpoint of the movement: "You want peace, finally you take guns to find it. Use drugs for opening your mind so everything will come inside—now you think only where to get more smack" (120). The deterministic narrative that Karl outlines is then brought to life by Phoebe's guide, Nico, who shoots up next to Phoebe; rather than being horrified, Phoebe feels she has found the authenticity she sought: "Here was the underground world, here it was; after a lifetime of stolen glimpses, she was right in its midst" (121-2). But like the initial feeling she had in London, it does not last; Karl clumsily attempts to sleep with her, so she escapes to her hostel where she has met some American backpackers. While she was experiencing the "underground," they visited the Heineken Brewery and Anne Frank's House (127), a ludicrous juxtaposition that develops Egan's point from "Letter to Josephine," where being a tourist flattens signs and images into a single experience of travel.

After a week in Namur, Belgium, Phoebe moves on to Reims, France. Here, "she leaned back, basking in her own sophistication, wishing someone were here to see her in Reims, France, dining alone at an elegant restaurant" (135). She is beginning to see herself as a person separate from Faith, rather than trying to become her. After an encounter with an Italian theology student, Pietro—an experience at a cathedral which further accentuates the pilgrimage nature of her trip—Phoebe travels to Paris, where she resolves to make "the final crucial, leap" (150), which is still completely undefined; the authenticity she seeks is nebulous, and without any clear referent. In Paris, she decides to take the acid that Kyle gave her in the opening scenes, hoping this will help her make said leap. After initially enjoying the experience, her trip starts to become unpleasant, and then gets much worse when she looks into a window and sees Faith. Tripping, she converses with Faith, who tells her they are "two halves of an apple," and that Phoebe needs to "push" to "get across" (154). As Phoebe slams herself against the glass, the image of Faith implores her to keep pushing harder. This scene captures the impossibility of Phoebe realizing her nostalgia for the present; Faith can exist only as an image, and as hard as Phoebe may push to reach her, time has passed—she notes that "we are the same age"—and, quite simply, Faith is dead (154). Phoebe's failed attempt to reach this image of Faith by slamming herself against the glass represents the broader inertia of an era stuck looking backwards; this scene literalizes how Phoebe's understanding of the sixties is a reflection of her imagination, not of reality. She realizes the "crucial leap" she has tried to make is impossible, and she destroys Faith's postcards by throwing them in the Seine. Staring in the hotel mirror afterwards, she is enraged when "a freakish face, a ritual mask carved in her image but her own face, not Faith's" stares back at her (162). She is slowly becoming her own person, and in doing so, she fears that "I've killed her," and punches the mirror, "shattering her own startled look into several bright pieces" (162). Phoebe literally shatters her image of herself, as it no longer reflects Faith back at her; from this moment onwards, her image of Faith is gradually shattered more and more, as Phoebe slowly becomes a person who does not define herself as the twin or shadow of Faith.

From Activism to Terrorism

After her experiences in Paris, Phoebe travels to Berlin to visit the house of Kyle's friend. Here, in a coincidence worthy of Dickens, Phoebe finds Wolf housesitting with his fiancée. It is notable that Kyle, in providing the acid that leads to her revelations in Paris and in offering the address of a friend in Berlin where Wolf lives, is the kind of plot contrivance that rarely appears in Egan's later, more developed fiction. Wolf has changed; Phoebe says to him, "you look different . . . I don't know, respectable" (171). Wolf responds, "It's a different world," and once he joins the narrative, Phoebe's image of Faith's life is completely transformed by what she learns, not only about her sister's actions, but also about the late 1960s and the experiences that Wolf shared with Faith. In describing the transition from counterculture to terrorism, Egan depicts Faith as someone particularly vulnerable to the demands of the developing image culture.

Faith's understanding of herself as an image can be traced to her childhood. As a child, Faith is adored by her father, and he paints her constantly. Faith, in turn, grows to love images of herself: "she'd craved any glimpse she could catch of her own life reflected back at her" (27). She always seeks to be the most dramatic image possible: leaping from the highest diving board, or swimming out so far to sea that no one can see her. Faith lives out her life under the constant gaze of her father, and she grows to need this approval even after his death. Phoebe also remembers incidents from Faith's childhood that foreshadow the violence to come; Faith stabs herself in the thigh with some garden shears to get her own way, and she is inconsolable after shooting a rabbit while hunting. That she "failed somehow to realize that firing at a flash of brown fur would lead to something dying" points ahead to her failure to realize that a bomb could kill someone (36). When she stabs herself, "Phoebe saw in her sister's face a kind of wonderment at the power of what she had done. It was spring 1966. That fall Faith would start high school, and within a year would be immersed in what had become, in retrospect, the sixties" (26). Egan sets Faith up as being particularly susceptible to the pressures of a movement that lived in the spotlight, where every action was always news. While this depiction of the sixties completely occludes the important role that manipulating the media had in achieving political progress in the Civil Rights Movement, Egan's focus is specifically on the counterculture. As Wolf says to Phoebe, "It was all about watching ourselves happen" (183), and it is this metafictional understanding of themselves as the narrators and protagonists of history that characterizes Egan's depiction of countercultural movements. As Gitlin notes, America's youth were "visible as never before" due to being constantly the subject of journalism, particularly television journalism (*Sixties* 192). Egan often cites Gitlin's argument that the counterculture rose as a response to the Vietnam War. Regardless of how true this is, what is important here is how this concept deeply influences the construction of this text. Similarly, Wolf remembers the trigger for their trip being precisely the events they were reading about in the news. After "the bombings of Cambodia, after everything we'd done to stop the war," and the Kent State shootings, they felt "a level of evil you just couldn't cope with" (213). It was these events that triggered their desire to go to Europe, to see if they could effect change there.

When Phoebe arrives, Wolf takes her to the castle that was used as a basis for Sleeping Beauty's castle in the Disney film, and she realizes it was the castle "she'd spent hours of her childhood trying to crayon" (185). Wolf discusses the sad history of the castle, a vanity project of mad King Ludwig that bankrupted the state when it was built. Subsequently, the commercialized, Disney image of this castle has replaced this complex history, and in this sense the castle is a synecdoche for the 1960s: the revisions of the decade's history have packaged it into a consumable past, one in which tourists go to Haight Street, and many of the more contentious aspects of its various dissident and revolutionary movements have been obscured or ignored. Indeed, one of the key figures of the era, Che Guevara, is having his story packaged and sold by Phoebe's mother and her boyfriend, Jack Lamont, a film producer. But *Sleeping Beauty* has a broader resonance; released in 1959, it can be seen as an allegory for the awakening of the postwar American youth, and to point ahead to the tumultuous decade that was to come. The contradictions of San Francisco's hippie hotspots, King Ludwig's castle, and Che Guevara's life are shown by Egan to be resolved by a commercialization of this heritage; all contradictions are resolved by a staged authenticity, pre-packaged and sold to those looking to consume these images.

After a short time at Wolf's apartment Phoebe resolves to go to Corniglia to see where Faith killed herself. Wolf says he will go with her, which at first seems out of caring, but his motive is revealed to be that he was actually with Faith at the end and knows much more than he has told Phoebe. In recounting Faith's path to planting a bomb and her eventual suicide, Wolf provides Phoebe with the leap she is looking for. In one of her postcards, Faith theorizes that the world is concealed from view by "velvet ropes," like those found in museums, which hold people back from seeing the true backstage, the authentic reality of what is happening (152). Wolf's characterizes the era as one of constantly looking for the places they read about in the news, but never quite finding them. However, Wolf tells people that he "has no answers, only questions" about the period, and he believes himself to be a "bystander, beginning to end" (184). He is another example of someone who could not make what they were seeing on the news tally with their own experiences, and so who thought they must have missed what has since come to be understood as the sixties. His and Faith's experiences in Europe are much the same as Phoebe's. Faith had a bulletin board full of newspaper clippings, and when Phoebe tries to take them down—stories on the Tet Offensive, the March on the Pentagon, and the Kennedy assassination—they "crumbled like ash in her hands" (77). Wolf notes to Phoebe that he always needed glasses; he just never wore them—"my blurred youth" (171). It is in this blurry world that he and Faith traveled across Europe, trying to see behind the "velvet ropes" that Faith felt were hiding the authentic world she sought.

However, the only act of countercultural activism Wolf and Faith carry out is to throw pillow feathers from the Eiffel Tower. While Wolf acknowledges he will never forget this moment, the act is symbolic, a spectacle, and devoid of consequences. In Berlin, Faith found what she was looking for; a friend, Inge, tells Faith and Wolf about the Red Army Faction (RAF), and the role of former journalist Ulrike Meinhof in popularizing the group. Meinhof's position in the RAF is interesting for two reasons. First, in moving from journalism to radical activism and often terrorism, Meinhof represents the story Egan wishes to tell about the interdependent relationship between the media and radical activism. The other reason that Meinhof is so notable is for her gender, which, in the popular imagination, became a defining feature of these left-wing groups. In *Baader-Meinhof and the Novel: Narratives of the Nation / Fantasies of the Revolution, 1970–2010* (2012), Julian Preece, one of the few critics to discuss *The Invisible Circus,* albeit briefly, situates the novel within a broader literary and cultural history regarding Baader-Meinhof and the many groups they inspired. Preece notes that *The Invisible Circus* appears to be the last non-German novel to discuss the left-wing terrorism that dominated German life across the 1970s (interestingly, the last pre-9/11 American novel about terrorism will be the focus of the next chapter, as it was Egan's *Look at Me*). Preece explains that when Andreas Baader was broken out of prison, of the six who rescued him in his dramatic, televisual escape—which involved leaping from a rooftop—five of the gang were women (26). Preece goes on to show that while this was not typical of future events, images such as these lent themselves well to literature and film. Nevertheless "the female terrorist is rarely idealized, demonized, or eroticized in male fiction; far more often, she is domesticated, thus disarmed and rendered harmless" (27). This domestication can be seen outside of Baader-Meinhof fiction and outside of "male fiction," such as in the ways Doris Lessing's *The Good Terrorist* (1985) follows Alice, the well-intentioned radical, at every administrative step as she sets up a squat in London. Similarly, when Faith joins these groups, at first she is denied any prominent role and merely does the shopping. When she is asked to help cut a fence with wire cutters during a bank robbery, she is unable to do so, which leads to the Baader-Meinhof group dropping her. The death she eventually causes is an accident; after planting a bomb in a picnic basket inside the Chamber Court in Berlin, a janitor who was not supposed to be there is killed by the explosion. It is the press attention that was sought by Faith and those in the movement that torments her, as Wolf explains: "The papers . . . went nuts with the story: working class guy gets cut down, you know, by these kids—anarchists, supposedly on his side" (302). The grief and guilt that Faith experiences afterwards eventually lead to her suicide.

Faith's actions connect her to a recurring trope that has formed over the last couple of decades: the female terrorist who unwittingly murders someone, often a janitor or blue-collar worker, and then regrets their actions. In Lessing's *The Good Terrorist,* Alice, although not herself responsible for the car bomb that kills her friend and numerous others, is nonetheless affiliated with the group, and accepts their actions as necessary. In Dana Spiotta's *Eat the Document,* Mary Whittaker is hiding after a bombing—which, in a twist on the trope, she was the central figure in setting up—has gone wrong, while in Rachel Kushner's *The Flamethrowers* (2013) Reno falls into being a part of the Italian Red Brigade movement. Faith's actions, foreshadowed by the surprise she felt that hunting would involve killing animals, places her into a broader literary tradition of being almost naively duped into murder and then struggling to live with the consequences. The authenticity she sought with this group leads her to partake in a terrorist act, one which drives her to suicide. Her name is particularly fitting here, as she has lost her faith in the nebulously defined movement, and in 1970, at the literal end of the 1960s, she kills herself. While there is some debate over when what has come to be known as "the Sixties" truly ended—Mark West posits 1975, when the Vietnam war ended and the Symbionese Liberation Army and Patty Hearst affair concluded (178)—Faith's death does at least signal a waning belief in the political potential of the activism that dominated the era.

The other feature of Faith's radicalization is the way it is bound up with images and the media. As Margaret Scanlan notes in her study of literature and terrorism, popular journalism found a natural ally in the actions of terrorists: "the blunted language of a debased politics is the language of newspapers and television" (80). Egan suggests that the violent acts that Faith finds herself involved in were the logical conclusion of a time when Wolf admits to Phoebe, "We were news. Whatever we did felt so big, so unbelievably powerful, almost like it was happening in retrospect" (271). After taking part in the bank robbery with the Baader-Meinhof group, Faith is sent out to buy newspapers so the group can see themselves in the news; they never have to count the money they have stolen because they are told by the newspapers.[5] Wolf also confesses his jealousy, brought about by Faith's newfound infamy: "She was in the world, you know? Out there doing something real, and here I was, following the story in the fucking newspaper" (229). However, Faith's experiences included not just the spectacle of the bank robbery, but also the domestic acts and day-to-day drudgery of being in hiding. Egan suggests that the relationship between activism and the media reporting on such events pushes some people to these spectacular acts of violence, which they regret. But, like Faith's postcards, such reporting is only part of the story. *The Invisible Circus* traces the ways the radical fervor of the 1960s led to violence, and how violence was brought about by a mutually dependent relationship between the media and those "watching themselves" as part of the movement.

Looking to the Future

Egan uses Phoebe's journey to represent a broader societal shift from constantly looking backward to finally looking forward. In the concluding section of the novel, Phoebe notices a new atmosphere where the culture has moved on from a sense of having "missed it" to the promises of a technological future that "filled them with hope" (337). The 1978 setting is on the precipice of technological changes which Egan will explore in depth in her next three novels before returning to historical fiction with *Manhattan Beach*. The person who symbolizes this change in *The Invisible Circus* is Barry, Phoebe's millionaire brother who runs a software company in Palo Alto. On a family picnic, Barry "pulled from his briefcase a miniature Sony tape player with tiny earphones attached, inspired, he said, by the chairman's wish to listen to opera while skiing" (325). The tape player most clearly connects this novel to *Goon Squad*, but also to the atomized technological future envisioned in *Look at Me* and the digital dislocations Egan depicts in *The Keep*. Phoebe is amazed by the technology, and realizes that the past she has been chasing, the nostalgia for the present she has been trying to capture, "was gone. But something also was beginning" (337). Egan's historical novel is situated on the precipice of the 1980s, and the technological and financial innovations that will dominate America over the next decade: "the clean, inarguable power of machines, the promise of extraordinary wealth" (337). The failed promise of the "hope" of "transformation" that Phoebe feels "flutter beneath the city" is the topic of Egan's next three novels (337).

4

Look at Me

After the relative success of *The Invisible Circus,* Egan began research for a new novel centered on modeling. Her attempts to look behind the curtain of the industry were ignored, as no agency wanted to give a largely unheard-of novelist unfettered access. But, luckily, she was offered the chance to write a piece for the *New York Times Magazine,* the first article of what is now a long nonfiction career. After eight months of research, "James is a Girl" was published on February 4, 1996. This article details the life of Jaime King, who at the time was a rising star of the modeling world. After this initial piece, Egan penned an essay for *Salon* about her teenage struggles with anorexia (1997) and was given a yearly assignment by the *Times Magazine.* Egan's nonfiction has yet to be collected into a single volume, but she is a journalist of great skill and a generous reviewer of the fiction of her contemporaries. Moreover, there is a symbiotic relationship, which is particularly apparent in *Look at Me,* between her nonfiction and her fiction.

Look at Me, published on September 18, 2001, is a hugely ambitious and multilayered work of what Egan terms "futurism," detailing the vacuity and vapidity of American life at the turn of the millennium (Lopate). Egan stated in 2018 that it is her "favorite" of her novels: "It's flawed, but it's the most ambitious in my opinion. I have not topped it" (Vorda). Indeed, it is the novel I always recommend to others when they ask where to start, as I believe it is her finest novel to date. A National Book Award finalist in 2001 (losing to Jonathan Franzen's *The Corrections*), it is, like Octavia Butler's *Parable of the Sower* (1993) or David Foster Wallace's *Infinite Jest* (1996), an oddly prescient work. *Look at Me* features the terrorist figure Z/Michael West, a character who would become disturbingly pertinent in light of the events of September 11, 2001, which happened just a week before *Look at Me* hit the shelves. In later editions, Egan felt compelled to add an afterword where she explains Z "remains an imaginative artefact of a more innocent time" (419). But Z is just one element of the uncanny prescience of *Look at Me,* as Egan depicts a near future that looks a lot like the present. The latter half of the novel introduces an online platform called Ordinary People in which people film their everyday lives for others to view (198). This section is not only reflective of reality television—which began to boom around this time, the first episode of *Survivor* airing in 2000—but it also presages Instagram influencers and sites like GoFundMe, or, in having a live birth filmed, sites like BirthTUBE. Building on the themes of *The Invisible Circus, Look at Me* explores the ways in which images are constructed, managed, and maintained. In *Look at Me,* Egan depicts the ways that the desire for authenticity has driven everyone to new levels of stagedness, of what Egan herself calls the "pseudo-events" that define contemporary existence. The near future she imagines is also representative of what Shoshana Zuboff labels "surveillance capitalism," a topic that Egan continues to explore in *Goon Squad.*

Look at Me follows the lives of two Charlottes: Charlotte Swenson is a middling catalog model who lives in New York, and Charlotte Hauser is a teenager in Rockford, Illinois. Egan contrasts these dual settings throughout to show the divergence between Midwest towns and coastal megacities like New York. We first meet the older Charlotte after a horrific car accident that has led her to have facial reconstructive surgery, rendering her unrecognizable to even those who know her. As a result of this operation her skull is held together by 80 titanium screws. The accident, just outside of Rockford, Illinois, was partly inspired by a car accident Egan herself had as a teenager while driving in San Francisco with her mother (Vorda). After Charlotte falls into alcoholism and struggles to get her life back on track, the novel ends with her reenacting the crash—in a manner partly resembling J. G. Ballard's postmodern classic *Crash* (1976)—for Ordinary People, and eventually selling the rights to her identity to the production company. Between these two crashes, Charlotte befriends and becomes romantically involved with a private detective, Anthony Halliday, a recovering alcoholic who is investigating Z. She also meets Irene Maitlock, an adjunct professor of comparative literature who initially claims to be a reporter for the *New Yorker* and to be writing a story about Charlotte. Really, Irene is initially working for Halliday, hoping to find out what Charlotte knows about Z. Irene's specialty is how literary genres influence human behavior, so her studies are essentially of figures like Halliday, who is shown reading Raymond Chandler's *The Long Goodbye* in one scene (148). Irene becomes the author of Charlotte's online life and ends up as the first "new new journalist" in the dystopian near future that concludes the novel (415).

Charlotte Hauser is the daughter of the older Charlotte's estranged best friend from childhood, Ellen Metcalf. Ellen is frustrated to be back in Rockford, and feels guilty for an extra-marital affair, so much so that she blames this relationship for the leukemia suffered by her teenage son, Ricky. Ellen's husband, Harris, runs a polling company in which he uses Rockford as the barometer of American values. The younger Charlotte begins a relationship with a man she knows as a math teacher named Michael West, but who is really Z, the former Hezbollah activist who is now mysteriously on the run, and who was in the car with the older Charlotte when she crashed. The younger Charlotte's story is another instance of a teenager coming of age in Egan's work; indeed, the novel begins with the older Charlotte remembering her teens in Rockford, and the sex she had with Ellen that led to them drifting apart. As with all of Egan's fiction except *The Keep,* the sexuality of young women is a central part of *Look at Me.* Through these intertwining plots—the events of which take place over less than a year—Egan develops a rich depiction of America at the turn of the millennium, one saturated with images, a thirst for authenticity, and on the brink of a new technological future. As well as a Lynchian sense of unreality, the story abounds with references to Lynch's popular television series *Twin Peaks,* such as a sawmill and a character called Leland. Indeed, from this perspective, *The Invisible Circus* also shares a similar structure to *Twin Peaks,* with Faith fulfilling the role of Laura Palmer, whose seemingly bright and perfect life hides a dark underworld. *Look at Me* is also Egan's most DeLilloian novel, indebted to DeLillo's *White Noise* (1985) in its satire and to *Underworld* (1997) in its scope and ambition. There is a brief nod to DeLillo's image of the "most photographed barn in America" from *White Noise,* where crowds are drawn "as if by a heavenly sign" to the recreation of Charlotte's crash (395). *Look at Me* has somehow been largely critically overlooked, despite how much it appears to have predicted about contemporary American life.

In one of the few critical articles to discuss *Look at Me,* Adam Kelly argues "few writers" have responded to postmodernism and postmodernity "more directly" than Egan ("Beginning" 393). He asserts this is "one of the main projects" of *Look at Me* (399). Kelly situates this novel as a transitional text, one that processes and responds to the postmodern concerns articulated by Fredric Jameson regarding the waning of affect, and Jameson's other canonical definitions of the postmodern era. Kelly argues that *Look at Me* thematizes the struggle to understand postmodern fiction as the product of a specific historical moment, and yet "not to forget the lessons of postmodernism, however liberating such forgetting may sometimes feel" (415). Stephanie Lambert, meanwhile, situates *Look at Me* as a rejection of the movement known as "the New Sincerity" (the definitions of which Kelly is perhaps the key figure in devising), and places Egan's novel in opposition to David Foster Wallace's collection *Brief Interviews with Hideous Men* (1999). Lambert contends that *Look at Me* "exposes the misogyny that underlies the quest for sincerity and foregrounds the specifically gendered consequences of the forms of value extraction inaugurated by neoliberal capital" (3). Lambert posits that while Egan depicts a world in which "the body is subject to ever-more intensive exploitation, its inherent elusiveness imbues it with the potential for resistance" (15). David Wylot focuses on the trauma of Charlotte's crash and explores *Look at Me* alongside Tom McCarthy's *Remainder* (2005) through the lens of trauma studies. All of these readings provide compelling insights into the novel, but rather than looking back at how Egan responds to postmodernity or how her fiction compares to that of contemporaries such as Wallace or McCarthy, here I read *Look at Me* as a transitional text for many cultural developments seen in America over the last two decades. While I argued in the previous chapter that in *The Invisible Circus* Egan depicts a metafictional history, with the protestors of the 1960s understanding themselves as images and as news, in *Look at Me* this logic has been extended across the populace, and every American is asking everyone to "look at me." In his book on photography, *Camera Lucida: Reflections on Photography* (1980), Roland Barthes contends that "the 'private life' is nothing but that zone of space, of time, where I am not an image, an object. It is my *political* right to be a subject which I must protect" (15). However, in *Look at Me,* Egan suggests technological developments and a cultural obsession with being looked at means this right has been erased for many Americans; the desire to be looked at and recognized as an autonomous being has in itself removed the ability to be a subject.

Mirrors and Doubling

While Egan did have her own brief foray into modeling in the 1980s, the research for "James is a Girl" clearly influences her depiction of modeling in *Look at Me.* In this article Egan observed that models took on a new significance in 1990s America: "Certainly models are this decade's contribution to our already crowded celebrity pantheon. They are what rock stars were to the 70's and visual artists were to the 80's" (1996). Here, Egan traces a history of celebrity and situates models as representative of the era: "Models are perfectly suited to a culture obsessed with fame for its own sake. Appearing in the media is their job—their images are their stock in trade. They are famous for being famous." This final line is drawn from Daniel Boorstin's *The Image: A Guide to Pseudo-Events in America* (1961), a sociological work about the centrality of images to American culture that Egan often cites as important in the development of *Look at Me.* While there have been more recent explorations of this phenomenon, such as Guy Debord's *Society of the Spectacle* (1967) or Jean Baudrillard's *Simulacra and Simulation* (1981), Egan prioritizes Boorstin's insights because they were made before many of the developments regarding the ubiquity of the image came to pass; in fact, she argues it is "a book that everyone in America should read every few years" (Birnbaum). Boorstin characterizes 1960s America as an "Age of Contrivance" (255), when Americans "want and . . . believe these illusions because we suffer from extravagant expectations" (3). As Phoebe, Faith, and Wolf experience in *The Invisible Circus,* the image of the world projected in the media raises expectations of reality. Each of these images are what Boorstin terms "a pseudo-event." He defines a pseudo-event as a false happening that is planned with the intention of being reproduced, but which is only tenuously related to an "underlying reality" (11). In many ways, modeling is the paradigmatic example of the pseudo-event: each picture is planned, it raises expectations, and the images are always produced with the intention of being reproduced. Or, as Egan describes this process in "James is a Girl": "So teen-age girls simulate an adulthood they have yet to experience, for the consumption of adult women who then feel dogged by standards of youth and beauty they will never meet. Welcome to image culture's hall of mirrors" (1996). This hall of mirrors is also drawn from Boorstin, who defines the narrowing reality caused by the ever-expanding world of pseudo-events thus: "we mark the boundaries of our world with a wall of mirrors" (255). Throughout *Look at Me,* and in the title itself, the notion of mirrors narrowing or restricting experience is central to many of the characters' lives. As Egan said to Vendela Vida, *Look at Me* is about "twinning or doubling in the context of image culture, asking how reflections of us affect our inner visions of ourselves." Through her accident and painful reconstruction (many details of which are inspired by Naomi Wolf's discussion of plastic surgery in *The Beauty Myth* [1990]), Charlotte is unique in that she no longer recognizes herself in the mirror, and no one else recognizes her either (Fradkin).[1]

One half of the plot builds from the older Charlotte's attempts to reestablish herself in the world of modeling through an agent, Oscar, who, despite having previously slept with Charlotte and having been friends with her for a long time, no longer recognizes her. Even Charlotte does not recognize herself, and once her bandages are removed, she talks to her new self in the mirror: "This is your Charlotte, and you must take good care of her so she'll grow up to be a beautiful girl, and live an extraordinary life" (28). She makes this speech to herself just after meeting the younger Charlotte in her family home, and she talks to her own new face like a child she must nurture. Indeed, mirrors and reflections are central to much of *Look at Me*; for instance, the older Charlotte discusses her brief college experiences as University of Illinois, Urbana-

Champaign, when she used to go to Chicago and stare at "the mirrored room," an area she imagines full of celebrities, "a place I had never seen and knew little about" (132). Like the glass Phoebe smashes against to reach Faith in *The Invisible Circus,* or the velvet ropes across Europe that Faith longs to transgress, this mirrored room, this imagined area of authenticity, is where Charlotte longs to be. Mirrors and doubles proliferate throughout the novel, from the doubled Charlottes, to the two names of Michael West/Z, to the way the older Charlotte believes she can see people's "shadow selves" (83). Some events also happen twice, such as Charlotte's crash, versions of which both begin and end the book. The early scene where Charlotte talks to herself in the mirror foreshadows the events at the end, as she does sell the "Charlotte" she addresses in that mirror to the production company. The idea that reflections capture an image rather than the essence of a person is suggested by the many characters who are struggling with the mirrored understanding of themselves.

Indeed, another central character in the plot is Moose Metcalf, a precarious academic—his title is "Adjunct Assistant Adjunct Professor of History" (108)—at the (fictional) community college in Rockford, Winnebago College, the name of which indicates the transience and precarity of Moose's position. Moose, the brother of Ellen, is a character Egan adores; she has called him "my favorite character" (Lukin), and she confesses the editing process of *Look at Me* involved "removing some Moose" (Lopate). Moose struggles with mental illness, and in a previous teaching experience at Yale, he tested his students with a moral problem that involved an actual bomb, an act that derailed what was a promising academic career. Egan has pointed out this was all conceived before the Unabomber was discovered to be an academic, another instance of *Look at Me* seeming to presage reality (Hogan). Moose has what Egan calls a "Big Theory" that fuels much of the plot (Lukin). He has published a book about the effects wrought by the perfection of clear, reflective glass in Murano, Italy, around 1300. He muses that the most shocking revelation of these reflections was people's own "physicality . . . Lacan's mirror phase wrought large upon whole villages" (109). In Jacques Lacan's theories, the mirror stage is a foundational stage of development when infants recognize themselves as an other—which Lacan describes as "the transformation that takes place in the subject when he assumes an image" (4). The mirror stage leads to the transition of the self from the "*Innenwelt,*" meaning the inner-world, to a recognition of the self as part of the "*Umwelt,*" or the environment (6). In this moment of recognition of the self as an image, as part of an environment, the self is forever afterwards defined by the "donned armor of an alienating identity that will mark his entire development with its rigid structure" (6). In Moose's history, as Kelly points out, this is a historical event, one that did not happen until the technology allowed it to happen ("Beginning" 410). Moose believes the world is now blinded by the proliferation of images, and that "the world's blindness exceeded that of medieval times before clear glass, except that the present blindness came from *too much sight,* appearances disjoined from anything real, afloat upon nothing, in the service of nothing, cut off from every source of blood and life" (109). In Moose's materialist history, the pseudo-events of the reflection, of the image, have gradually built from the medieval period to the world he finds himself in now, where everyone dons the armor of their perception of themselves.

Moose's grand theory does lead to some off-putting and absurd behaviors. For instance, because he "believed adamantly in regulating the imagery one allowed to penetrate oneself," he rarely looks at people directly (112). As Lambert notes, he drives a station wagon that he believes "is a source of authenticity" (11), and as a miniscule rebellion against the atomization of experience in turn-of-millennium America, he refuses to own a computer or a phone. He begins to tutor the younger Charlotte, his niece, about the history of Rockford, as he is working on an extensive book about the city in which he argues that it is paradigmatic of America writ large. When looking at his maps of Rockford, he expounds: "the narrative of industrial America [is] told in these glyphs: a tale that began with the rationalization of objects through standardization, abstraction and mass production, and concluded with the rationalization of human beings through marketing, public relations, image consulting and spin" (183). Moose's belief that Rockford is representative of a broader history of America mirrors the beliefs of his brother-in-law, Harris. Harris is a largely dislikeable character who represents the world of "public relations, image consulting and spin," and he is initially resistant to the idea of Moose tutoring his daughter. However, his conclusions about Rockford as a mirror of America are similar to Moose's. He is a pollster, and he believes Rockford is "the center of the world. The place everyone turned to learn what American voters and moviegoers and worshipers, investors and sports fans, dieters, parents, cooks, drivers, smokers, hospital patients, music lovers, homebuilders, drinkers, gardeners really cared about" (235). Harris believes he "had those answers. Or knew how to find them" (235). In this world of mirrors, Moose's ideas are the imperfect reflection of Harris's business; both of them believe Rockford to be a mirror of America, but in completely different ways and to serve completely different ends.

Another mirroring can be found in the figure of Z, who has made Rockford his home after his car crash while driving with Charlotte from New York. Z studies television in order to pass as an American, as a mirror of American life: "He watched the programs that everyone watched, and when he wasn't watching, he listened—for accents, facts, common knowledge. Sometimes he had trouble distinguishing between TV events and real ones; certain things on TV could not happen in real life, even in America" (124). Z mirrors everyone he meets, and seeing typical mannerisms and behaviors reflected back, no one suspects his intentions. Z's behavior is another illustration of how pseudo-events proliferate; he mirrors the behavior and speech of the fictional television shows with the ultimate aim of blending in so well that he can then create violent spectacles of his own, which will feed back into the same television from which he has learned his behavior. Intriguingly, Egan has pointed out that Z and Charlotte are products of the same culture: "I wanted to include a terrorist because terrorism of this nature is a byproduct of image culture" (Miller). In this sense, Z is a dark reflection of Charlotte's modeling, as his planned actions, like Charlotte's career, are "completely dependent on the media" (Miller). Moreover, toward the end of *Look at Me,* Z considers moving to Hollywood and selling his story, "to exchange plots for plots" (313). He considers how his story is one of "self-discovery," and "one man's personal history," features which make him distinctly "*American!*" (310–312). He withdraws from this idea, dismissing these thoughts as the result of the "conspiracy" of American cultural hegemony. In his musings about America's obsession with personal history and his apocalyptic visions, Z mirrors the ideas of Moose; not only did Moose plan a sort of terroristic plot, but in teaching his niece, he observes, "it was the reigning habit of mind in this land without history . . . to fill the breach with *personal history,* that diminutive, myopic substitute" (288). Moose's grand theories have a series of mirrors throughout the novel, seen in both Harris's polling and Z's plotting.

Cultural Productions and Staged Authenticity

The television shows that Z consumes and attempts to mirror exemplify the influence of what MacCannell terms "cultural experiences." In his words, "The data of cultural experiences are somewhat fictionalized, idealized or exaggerated models of social life that are in the public domain, in film, fiction, political rhetoric, small talk, comic strips, expositions, etiquette and spectacles" (*The Tourist* 23). These products are what MacCannell calls "models," and he notes that by this he means "an embodied ideal," much like the world of mirrors that Egan describes as defining the uncanny realm of fashion modeling (24). MacCannell then argues that these models have an "influence," which he explains thus: "A bathing-suit model is a model; the desire for a real-life girlfriend that looks 'just like a model' is its influence" (24). In *Look at Me,* Charlotte wishes while planning her facial reconstructive surgery that she had some bad pictures of herself; she only has the model version of herself, and so the influence will be wrong for the surgeon: "The old pictures were no help; like all good pictures, they hid the truth" (32). Finally, MacCannell states that each cultural production is made by a medium, and that this is "an agency that connects a model and its influence" (*The Tourist* 24). Throughout *Look at Me,* there are characters who manage experience, who are the mediums that define what is influential. As MacCannell argues, "Cultural productions, then, are not merely repositories of models for social life; they organize the attitudes we have toward the models and life" (*The Tourist* 27). Egan's focus is on the management of these cultural productions, and how image culture organizes experience in a specific way.

In *Look at Me,* what is intriguing is how these cultural productions are constantly cast as attempts to depict authentic experience, but all of these cultural productions are staged—the novel is dominated by images of staged authenticity. As mentioned in the introduction, MacCannell built his concept of staged authenticity from Erving Goffman's arguments that the self is "a performed character," rather than "an organic thing that has a specific location" (*Presentation* 252). Goffman describes people as putting on a mask, their front, which contrasts with a backstage or off-screen world in which they manage themselves before stepping onto the stage. One clear example he gives of this, building from Simone de Beauvoir's example from *The Second Sex* (1953) of what happens when a male audience is absent, is that of women putting on makeup behind the scenes, and the public face being one that has been managed and planned (113). It would at first appear that Goffman's theories connect to Egan's novel; Charlotte believes she can access "shadow selves" of everyone around her, that she can see the real person behind each mask. However, this self-proclaimed ability is no more accurate than Danny's claims in *The Keep* that he can feel Wi-Fi, as Irene and Anthony Halliday have been lying to her since she met them. MacCannell's concept indicates that most images of authenticity are in fact staged, or managed, to make the viewer believe they are accessing a back region; he states that staged authenticity "involves the putative removal of barriers to perception between front and back regions" (*Ethics* 18). One example is a film that Charlotte watches during her recovery, "*The Making of the Making of,* a documentary about how documentaries were made about the making of Hollywood features" (78). This documentary is partly a satire of documentaries like *Hearts of Darkness: A Filmmaker's Apocalypse* (1991), which details the filming of *Apocalypse Now* (1979), and *Burden of Dreams* (1982), which captured the tempestuous filming of *Fitzcarraldo* (1982). But "*The Making of the Making of*" is one step further removed from the source material, showing the infinite regress of staged authenticity; once a back region is seen to be managed, a new layer of authenticity is sought.

The older Charlotte attempts to return to modeling and is surprised and delighted when she is hired by Italian *Vogue* for a shoot. Her agent, Oscar, details how the photographer, Spiro, has become the hottest photographer in New York following a show that was "an homage to Gordon Parks consisting of black-and-white photos of a sixteen-year-old gang leader called Honey B" (130). In this *Zoolander*-esque shoot—incidentally, a film released the same year as *Look at Me*—"Reviewers praised the show's gritty authenticity, its unblinking portraits of urban violence rendered in magisterial tableaux reminiscent of Goya" (130). In this passage, authenticity is defined in reference not to some source material, but to the photography of Gordon Parks and the paintings of Goya. The pseudo-events have once again led to more pseudo-events: another series is commissioned based on these pictures, this time featuring models "posing as gang members," with shots such as "Kate Moss holding a sawed-off shotgun to the head of a blindfolded and kneeling Amber Valetta" (130). This is a cultural production that pretends to access the backstage of New York life, but is in fact another staged image of authenticity.

Spiro's plans for Charlotte are again to stage an experience of authenticity; he wants to cut her face, and then photograph it bleeding. Once again revealing the influence of her journalism on her fiction, Egan has discussed the effects of her article on self-harm, "The Thin Red Line" (1997), on this scene (Hogan). Spiro frames this project as a desire for authenticity: "I'm trying to get at some kind of truth here, in this phony, sick, ludicrous world. Something pure. Releasing blood is a sacrifice. It's the most real thing there is" (144). Spiro's request is framed as a desire to stage an image of authenticity; he states that these pictures are an attempt to "cut through the shit to what's real and fundamental" (145). He is at once literalizing that process of cutting and also using it as a metaphor for the "phony, sick, ludicrous world." In *Camera Lucida,* Barthes argues that there are layers of comprehension when looking at a photograph. Barthes argues that "a photograph's *punctum,*" meaning its deepest layer, "is that accident which pricks me (but also bruises me, is poignant to me)" (27). Although it is eminently possible Egan is directly referencing Barthes here—as Nicholas Dames points out, she is part of the "Theory Generation"—what is important is how Spiro's photography literalizes this desire to capture this authentic *punctum.* While Charlotte does not let them cut her, the photograph Spiro desires is emblematic of a broader concern with staged authenticity throughout the novel. That it is a North Korean refugee who steps into Charlotte's place to be cut and photographed is further evidence that Spiro does not truly care for authenticity in service of any particular moral purpose—his only wish is to make his image into reality.

Another image of staged authenticity is found in Harris's polling. His belief that Rockford is "the center of the world" is a self-fulfilling prophecy. Once designated as such a place, Rockford becomes the stage for the authentic America that companies seek. This management of authenticity—something Egan has explored since her short stories "The Stylist" and "Emerald City"—dominates the latter half of the novel. After leaving Spiro's studio, Charlotte drunkenly attempts to jump from her apartment balcony in a tragicomic suicide attempt. She then resolves to turn her life around. She hires Victoria Knight, a "surgeon of reality," whose special skill is to promote people (194). Victoria is being followed by an NYU media studies student, Phillippe, who is writing about her work; as with *The Making of the Making of* documentary, the managers of the staging become a stage at some point, and so that stage is studied as the truly authentic subject. It is through Victoria that Charlotte is pointed toward Ordinary People, the online platform where people are paid to share their lives on their "PersonalSpace" (198). The brain behind this operation is Thomas Keene, one of Egan's most fascinating characters.

Thomas's plan is to create an online platform that, to readers two decades later, sounds much like a blend of reality television and social media. Thomas wishes to have a site that hosts people being filmed as they go about their everyday lives, hence the name Ordinary People. However, he also wants to have a few people who viewers may find more interesting, called "Extra Ordinaries," of which Charlotte would be one. He notes that the platform will encourage product placement, but that users will have to "go easy on that stuff, because authenticity is everything, here" (200). But this authenticity is staged and managed in order for Thomas to produce the effect he desires. Thomas believes people are craving authenticity; when Charlotte objects that it might be boring, he replies that "most of us are desperate for raw experience" (200). Interestingly, he puts this in the context of sightseeing being exhausted, claiming that the age of tourism may be over: "No one actually *makes* anything anymore, and our so-called experiences are about climbing Mount Kilimanjaro on our two-week vacations or snapping a picture of the Dalai Lama in Central Park" (200). Thomas then makes a speech that encapsulates the dilemma of staged authenticity that MacCannell defines: "But we're so powerfully aware of all the stuff we're missing! It creates this frustration, this craving to get out of ourselves. TV tries to satisfy that, books, movies—they try, but they're all so lame—so mediated! They're just not *real* enough" (200). Thomas's dream is an example of how, in Boorstin's terms, pseudo-events lead to further pseudo-events. Thomas once again invokes tourism as the context for Ordinary People: "I think the golden age of tourism is basically over, especially for Americans. The coral's dead or dying, you've got weird grass choking out the Med, you've got e-coli and flesh-eating diseases all over the place, you've got terrorists mowing people down in the Temple of Luxor" (261). He concludes, "I mean, at a certain point, how much are you willing to risk for a two-week vacation? So we're thinking ahead" (261). Thomas situates Ordinary People as a natural heir to tourism, which is exactly how MacCannell discusses this process: "A globally integrated system of values, protocols, and practices did not originate with the internet. It originated in response to the movements, motives, and needs of tourists and was largely realized by the midpoint of the twentieth century" (*The Tourist* xxiii). Thomas's platform is, in many ways, a vast expansion of the sightseeing that tourists seek, and that Phoebe, Faith, and Wolf sought in *The Invisible Circus.*

By claiming to give unmediated access to people from across the globe, Thomas is prioritizing his version of authenticity above all other concerns. For example, Thomas explains that he will allow only one Ordinary to represent any given type of person: "Maybe two Ordinaries will sound similar—same fantasies, same family configuration, it happens—and one will have to go" (203). His business plan brings to mind what MacCannell terms "the ethics of sightseeing." By prioritizing authenticity in such a way, Thomas has completely obfuscated any ethical concerns. As MacCannell argues, "Accordingly, any belief in *authenticity*—that is, any notion that one might bypass the symbolic and enter into a complete, open, fully authentic relation with another subject—obviates questions of ethics. Authenticity as a substitute for ethics can be regarded with suspicion that it is either intentionally or unwittingly unethical" (*Ethics* 10). By prioritizing authenticity above all else—so that, in Thomas's words, "authenticity is the beginning and the end of this product"—Thomas overrides any concerns about the ethics of his project (255). Like Spiro's photography, this leads to the exploitation of others, and as Lambert persuasively argues, "a quest for the 'real' beneath the postmodern simulation can amount to a form of misogyny and violence" (2). The fact that these images of authenticity are managed and contrived is also lost on Thomas and Spiro, as they provide access to an image of a backstage, a staged version of authenticity with dubious ethics.

As part of the management of his subjects, Thomas demands that they all have their lives scripted in diaries that are released as if they are the real, unmediated thoughts of the person being filmed. For this task, Charlotte brings in Irene Maitlock. Irene and Thomas discuss how to present Charlotte's story, and Thomas says, "I'm not saying make it up—I'm saying find the connections. Show us the buried logic" (256). He then states he does not want a Raymond Carver story, and Irene and Thomas settle on "the nineteenth century" as a model, and Thomas elaborates, "Hardy. The Brontes. Tolstoy. Sad things happen but they happen for a reason" (256). During this exchange, Thomas keeps referring to Charlotte as "her," even though she is in the room. When she challenges him, he apologizes, and explains that this is a "habit from creative writing class" (254). Ordinary People, far from being a platform that provides unmediated access to its subjects, is heavily managed, scripted, and shaped to fit certain narratives. Thomas exploits history, art, his subjects, and everyone around him to make money. Ethics are not his concern; his priority is simply to make his product consumable and reproducible.

Thomas's lack of empathy or concern with ethics also comes to the fore in his remake of Charlotte's car crash. To borrow the awful term Tim Burton describes his 2001 remake of *Planet of the Apes,* Thomas "reimagines" this crash to be as dramatic and marketable as possible. At first, he tries to hire Ricky as the person who saves Charlotte from the car, because he is so photogenic; in the uncanny mirror of her life, he tries to make everyone involved more attractive. He is at first apprehensive when Ricky suggests his sister for the role, but he is then delighted when he finds out the younger Charlotte shares a name with the person whose crash he is reimagining. Thomas's management of the recreation of a historical event suggests that history does, to paraphrase Marx, happen first as tragedy and then as farce. Like Spiro, he makes a profit from people desperate for exposure, and he uses their need for capital to make capital for himself. Before signing up, Charlotte considers what options she has: "In rebellion, I reviewed the list of other things I could sell: apartment, clothing, sectional couch. They were only things; first one, then another, then another. Then they would all be gone. But a story was invisible, infinite, it had no size or shape. Information. It could fill the world or fit inside a fingernail" (208). She has nowhere else to turn; she has been reduced to bagging groceries, and so she begins to sell information about herself to make money.

Surveillance Capitalism: The Mirrored Room Becomes the Mirrored World

Thomas's vision is representative of a specific cultural logic that has come to dominate twenty-first century American life. As well as representing a "more innocent time," a pre-9/11 moment, *Look at Me* also points ahead to what Shoshana Zuboff defines as surveillance capitalism: "Surveillance capitalism is not technology: it is a logic that imbues technology and commands it into action. Surveillance capitalism is a market form that is unimaginable outside of the digital milieu, but it is not the same as the 'digital'" (15). This logic creates a world in which every aspect of behavior is monitored, recorded, and turned into data. This data is then used to sell products. But, as Zuboff describes, "surveillance capitalists discovered that the most-predictive behavioral data come from intervening in the state of play in order to nudge, coax, tune, and herd behavior toward profitable outcomes" (8). Thomas's vision is representative of the beginnings of this logic. As Zuboff notes, "surveillance capitalism was invented by a specific group of human beings in a specific time and place. It is not an inherent result of digital technology, nor is it a necessary expression of information capitalism" (85). Moreover, far from an authentic product for and by the people, Ordinary People exists because of funding from Time Warner and Microsoft. When Charlotte points out his backers, she observes, "I'd hit upon the one aspect of his venture that shamed him" (204). *Look at Me* captures a moment in the development of surveillance capitalism, and Ordinary People is the product of a specific logic—namely, the desire of those in charge of giant technology companies like Time Warner and Microsoft to maximize returns on their technological investments.

Thomas defends himself to Charlotte and Irene: "I invented this product, sure, but I'm not so unique—I'm part of a Zeitgeist. If I don't do it, someone else will" (263), and "It's going to happen with or without you" (263). Here, he obscures his personal responsibility for his subjects and for the product he has designed. He also claims, "If that's where it's going then I want to be there, making sure it's done responsibly" (263), situating himself as a shepherd of change rather than as an actor designing these cultural productions. Thomas's claims reflect what Zuboff calls the "inevitabilism" that permeates the logic of surveillance capitalism (343); as with his pursuit of authenticity being paramount in his product, these claims of platforms like Ordinary People being inevitable obfuscate the ethics of his endeavor. Moreover, in the figures of Mike and Ed, the farmers who are hired to dig the trench for the staged crash, Thomas gets to meet two people who are the victims of this attitude. Mike and Ed are happy to be "emancipated from the computer courses they'd been forced to take since the banks got their farms" (379). Egan's novel depicts a moment in history when the logic of surveillance capitalism was beginning to form, and then follows that logic through to the "futurism" of the last section. As people are being filmed and being viewed, their behavior is monitored for the market: "We want to get people in their natural environments doing exactly what they would normally do, but if companies are willing to pay them to use the products they've been using all their lives, I say, why the hell not?" (200). The other myth is that of a choice; Thomas rejects that this is like George Orwell's *1984*, as "this is not only a hundred percent voluntary, obviously, but the whole thing is *about* freedom—freedom to communicate your experiences!" (258). As indicated in the previous section, Charlotte is out of options, and this venture is not really voluntary at all.

Charlotte experiences what it is like to become one of the products of surveillance capitalism. She is interviewed by Irene, who makes notes about Charlotte's life. In reading these notes, Charlotte begins to surveil and monitor her own behavior: "I made a mental note not to refer to the couch again in Irene's presence" (275). In the final scenes of the novel, when they are recreating the crash, Charlotte remarks on the intrusive nature of the narrative voice—represented in the text with a typewriter-like typescript—which she is now hearing as she sees her own life from the perspective of a viewer, as content to sell. Irene is documenting everything she does, such as the nicknames her young nieces call her. This narrative voice, this self-surveillance, actually stops her drinking: "It was technically impossible to lose yourself in drink when a breathless narrator was panting into your ear . . . it was literally sobering" (332). In the dramatic recreation of the crash, Thomas commands Charlotte to "scream like you've never screamed in your life" (403). As she is dragged from the dramatic rain-splattered wreckage in the Rockford cornfield, "my mouth [became] a gigantic O that dredged up from within me a sound unlike any I had ever made before, or even heard" (405). She brings the drama that Thomas demands, and the recreation is an instance of what Jean Baudrillard terms the "hyperreal" in its intensity, while being almost completely divorced from its source material (28). Once she thinks of herself as a product, she begins to monitor and track how she behaves; she experiences the effects of the narrativization of the self that intrude once one feels oneself being surveilled or tracked. As she imagines herself as a storyline, there is one final mirroring between Charlotte and Z; as he thinks of his life as a Hollywood film, he monitors his behavior and modifies it to each setting. Charlotte polices her behavior once she feels her life is following a narrative, as she has a narrator explaining her actions. Ordinary People is unerringly prescient about Instagram influencers and the broader role that reality television has in American lives. The logics of surveillance capitalism are shown in *Look at Me* to be the product of a pretense of authenticity in which everyone is placed on a stage. By pretending to give the customer exactly what they want, without any regard for ethical considerations, Thomas is able to exploit a cultural desire for everyone to "look at me," and to monetize that urge.

In the final scenes of the novel, Charlotte is no longer Charlotte; just as she previously had to reinvent herself at the beginning by having her face redesigned, at the end she reinvents herself by selling her identity to Ordinary People. She does not give her new name, but Charlotte Swenson is now a digital entity: "Now a team of 3-D modelers and animators creates my likeness and superimposes her onto my balcony, my sectional couch, my kitchen, my bedroom" (414–415). Charlotte muses that pictures are trying to "capture the mysteries of ourselves," but that the mirrored room she always sought is "empty"

(415). In *Truman Show*–like fashion, her whole life has been on display, even her insides—"whose heart, with its yawning, shaggy caverns, is more recognizable to a majority of Americans (according to one recent study) than their spouses' hands" (411). As Boorstin argues, the pseudo-event breeds further pseudo-events, for as the desire for access to Charlotte grows stronger, it becomes even more hyperreal, a result Baudrillard partly defines as "an excessive transparency" (28). Charlotte's life is still written by Irene, but even that is no longer a secret: "As the first 'new new journalist,' Irene Maitlock is something of a legend, though by now scores of others have followed her example" (415). At the end of *Look at Me,* as throughout the novel, the underlying reality—Charlotte Swenson's life—becomes ever more distant. By selling her identity, Charlotte sells her reflection, the Charlotte she promised at the beginning of the novel she would give "an extraordinary life." As with the ending of *The Invisible Circus,* Egan looks to the future, but unlike her first novel, she sees not the potential of technology, but a digital dystopia. The topic of *The Keep* is precisely this digital milieu that she begins to explore throughout *Look at Me,* and in particular the Gothic nature of digital communication.

5

The Keep

Donald Trump communicated with his 88.8 million online followers, as of the time Twitter banned him from the platform, using the Twitter handle "@RealDonaldTrump" (Mak). By including the prefix "real" before his name, the moniker sought to reassure his readers of the authenticity of this account. However, this assertion of realness has often been called into question; Dan Scavino, Trump's social media director, is known to have often tweeted from this account, and so it was frequently unclear whether it was the "real" Trump tweeting his incendiary pronouncements (Draper). Moreover, there has been much debate over how many of his followers were real, with some estimates claiming up to 61% of his followers were actually bots (Campoy). Therefore, it was often not the "real" Donald Trump tweeting at all, and a majority of his audience was not real, either. While Trump's online decrees and Tweetstorms were presented as direct, authentic access to his inner thoughts and foibles—and reported by the media as such—there is an often-unacknowledged mystery over whether the authenticity of these tweets can ever be absolutely confirmed. Indeed, to broaden this point, much of online communication is infused with such uncertainty, and this is the central concern of Egan's third novel, *The Keep*. A metafictional Gothic novel set in an Eastern European castle in which Egan delights in playing with Gothic conventions, *The Keep* is also about this underlying uncertainty regarding the authenticity of all digital communication that Trump's Twitter account exemplifies. Through the supernatural, camp, and unstable world of the Gothic, Egan explores the crisis of legitimacy that marks any digital communication.

Egan was inspired to write *The Keep* after a trip to a Belgian castle, where "it felt revelatory and thrilling to be in a ruined castle and I thought: I have to write about this somehow" (Alford). After initially trying to write it as a "historical novel set in medieval times" (Alford), *The Keep* instead became a Gothic novel. But, as with every work in her oeuvre, the writing process was not easy; she even gave it the working title *A Short Bad Novel* (von Arbin Ahlander). In a 2001 interview with Ron Hogan, she discusses her preliminary plans for the follow-up to *Look at Me,* a structure which she largely kept to in the final version: "For a while, I wanted to do a Gothic story with a huge plot twist, but I haven't been able to sustain a sense of possibility about that idea, so I don't know where it's going to go anymore." As with *Look at Me,* she overcame these writing struggles partly through her journalistic endeavors. For instance, in "Lonely Gay Teen Seeking Same," she researched the secret lives of gay teenagers in burgeoning online communities. Here, she explains that one issue with "cyberrelationships" is "in the end, you're never really sure who they were in the first place." Moreover, she notes the tension inherent in online communication: "By fostering intimate exchanges stripped of all context, Internet dialogue combines too much information with too little. The possibility of deception is implicit." In this article, then, she was beginning to develop many of her ideas about the unknowability of online communication that she explores in *The Keep.* In 2003 she returned to her discussion of online dating more broadly in "Love in the Time of No Time," where she delved into the huge changes wrought by online dating. She concludes that "the long-term vision, here, looks like something out of a [Jorge Luis] Borges story: a virtual clearinghouse where potential lovers, friends, business associates, audience members and devotees of all forms of culture—invisible to one another in the shadowy cracks of cities around the world—are registered, profiled and findable." The connection to Borges's often convoluted and involuted narratives points ahead to *The Keep,* which has a metafictional structure that echoes Borges, Julio Cortázar, and other experimental writers.

But *The Keep* is also a self-consciously Gothic novel, and Gothic texts are often experimental in form. For example, by the end of the novel the reader discovers that one of the main characters has buried the very manuscript that forms this book. In its found-text structure, *The Keep* resembles classic Gothic works such as *The Turn of the Screw* (1898) as well as more recent metafictional Gothic horror novels like Mark Danielewski's *House of Leaves* (2001). To help her develop the voice of Ray, who largely narrates the novel, Egan turned to Ted Conover's *Newjack: Guarding Sing Sing* (2000), in which Conover details his experiences as a prison guard in New York, as well as Jimmy Lerner's *You Got Nothing Coming: Notes from a Prison Fish* (2002), a memoir based on Lerner's stint in a Nevada prison (Vida). By using such a voice, Egan set herself the challenge of having a narrator who is writing fiction for the first time. When Ray meets his writing instructor, Holly, near the end of the novel, they even discuss how his writing "is rough" and "needed work like everything does" (253). For her models of the Gothic, Egan says that she read "the usual suspects: Poe, James, Hawthorne, Joyce Carol Oates, Stephen King," as well as "the crazy old Gothic novels people don't read much anymore" (Vida) such as Horace Walpole's *The Castle of Otranto* (1764), Ann Radcliffe's *The Mysteries of Udolpho* (1794), and Matthew Lewis's *The Monk* (1796). The influence of Henry James's *The Turn of the Screw,* her "favorite" Gothic tale, is palpable in the uncertainty of what is happening throughout the novel (Vida). The first name of one of the main characters, Danny, is the same as the protagonist of King's *The Shining* (1977), and his last name, King, is an even clearer nod to this author. Another connection to King's classic is that the Gothic castle in which much of *The Keep* is set is in the process of becoming a secluded hotel with a violent history, similar to The Overlook Hotel. Egan also credits two other influential texts, ones which are less commonly read: "[Charles Maturin's] *Melmoth the Wanderer,* which is an absolutely wacky book inside a book inside a book, and Wilkie Collins's *The Woman in White,* which is one of the best thrillers I've ever read" (Vida). There is also, as Madison Smartt Bell argues in her glowing review, the evident influence of John Fowles's fantastical fiction, such as *The Magus* (1965). *The Keep* is therefore an intriguing blend of genres and styles, merging the prison memoir with the Gothic, the literary with the cinematic, and the generic with the experimental.

The Keep is, like *Melmoth,* a book within a book; the scenes in the castle are a part of story being told by Ray to his prison writing class. These strands are then connected in a final section told from the perspective of Holly, Ray's prison writing instructor, who visits the castle in which much of the novel is set. Egan describes the structure of *The Keep* as a romance: "The story of Ray and Holly, the love affair there, is a love of language. They each give each other the gift of writing. That's a gift that I somehow got, and that I'm grateful for. It's a very dewy-eyed book for me" (Yabroff). Indeed, Daniel Olson perceptively labels *The Keep* a "neo-Gothic romance" (329). While there were moments of the Gothic in all her earlier fiction—the twinning and doppelgangers of *The Invisible Circus* and *Look at Me* in particular—*The Keep* marked new ground for Egan, as it is undoubtedly and self-consciously a genre novel. Interestingly, she changed her editor and her literary agent for *The Keep,* because "there was a leap there that we could make aesthetically, my editor and I" (Lockwood). This relationship with genre characterizes all of her subsequent fiction. As I have written elsewhere, *The Keep* is part of the "genrefication" of contemporary American fiction, a process seen in the works of Michael Chabon, Colson Whitehead, Jonathan Lethem, Justin Cronin, Margaret Atwood, and many others (Moran). Egan's relationship to genre is, however, slightly different than many of these contemporaries; she told Robert Alford, "I know there's a way in which the tools that I'm really using as I write are emphases and extrapolation." As with creative writing programs, she works besides this development rather than consciously taking part of the shift to genre; as discussed in the introduction, Egan does not feel another "ism" is needed to define how fiction should be written. In *The Keep* the tools of the Gothic are used in a manner that resembles what Tzvetan Todorov describes as the Gothic subgenre of "the fantastic."[1] Through the methods of the fantastic, Egan emphasizes the staged authenticity that defines digital communication, and defamiliarizes her characters and readers from the unspoken assumptions of authenticity that define these connections.

Querying technological advancements is distinctly Gothic and has been a feature of the genre since its inception. As Jerrold Hogle notes, since Horace Walpole's *The Castle of Otranto,* recognized as the first modern Gothic novel, the Gothic "has thus come to connote a backward-leaning countermodernity lurking in both the emerging and recent stages of modern life" ("Introduction: Modernity" 4). In *The Keep,* Egan seeks to show certain underlying assumptions that define digital communication, a project that fits neatly with Hogle's definitions of Gothic fiction as operating to "undermine, and in that way 'haunt,' the assumption that the 'modern' has left behind any regressive tendencies that might impede its progress and fulfillment" ("Introduction: Modernity" 4). Throughout this Gothic novel Egan suggests she is deeply skeptical of the efficacy of digital platforms, a concern which culminates in the dystopian future she envisions in the Twitter short story "Black Box" six years later.

The Keep has two main settings: a castle/hotel situated in some hard-to-define area of Eastern Europe, and a prison in an undefined place in America. Both of these locales fit within what Hogle has listed as the expected settings of a Gothic novel, but they are rarely, if ever, seen together ("Introduction: The Gothic" 2). The castle has been purchased by Howard, a hugely successful bond trader who has retired in his thirties and purchased this castle, taking up residence in it along with his wife, Ann, their young child, Benjy, and their new baby. Once again in Egan's fiction, the accumulation of capital leads to the plot; Howard's capital functions in *The Keep* to account for the reason for this Gothic setting. He has a team of graduate students from Columbia and Dartmouth who are helping to establish the hotel as a retreat from the digital world. Working alongside Howard is "Mick," someone he met while in reform school, and whose full name is Raymond Michael Dobbs, the narrator for most of the book. Ray is writing the novel for his prison writing class, and he is in prison for the murder of Danny, Howard's estranged cousin whom he has invited out to the castle to help him set it up. Near the end of the novel, Ray escapes from prison with his unstable cellmate, Davis. At this point, Ray's writing instructor, Holly, a recovering meth addict who is rebuilding her life with her two young daughters, takes over the narration. In the final section, Holly—whose husband, Seth, a former musician, points ahead to the characters who populate *Goon Squad*—visits Howard's castle. This trip is partly a pilgrimage, like the tourist behavior MacCannell describes, in the hopes of seeing Ray again. Holly's need for this holiday, however, and the reason her mother is so keen for her to go, is so that she can recover from the tumultuous events of her life, such as the stillbirth of her son, Corey, as a result of her addiction. In a particularly Gothic moment, he is born with "a shrunken face like a mummy dug up after centuries" (232), and Holly keeps asking, "Can't we put him back?" (232). From the castle to the prison and then to Holly's home, every level of the narrative is permeated with Gothic tropes and references.

But Egan notes that the Gothic is identifiable not only by its darkness and horror; it also often contains the opposite, "the kind of fake medievalism of the Gothic . . . the sort of cheesiness, if you will, of that Gothic atmosphere," which Egan says appealed to her (Alford). Danny's appearance embodies this: he is a goth with "white skin Danny made even whiter with Johnson's baby powder," and "straight dyed-black hair an inch past his neck. A pewter hoop in one ear with a ruby stuck in it" (27). As well as Danny's carefully sculpted appearance, there is also the Baroness, the last holdout of the Von Ausblinkers, the family who owned the castle before Howard purchased it. She remains in the keep of the castle that gives the novel its name, and she speaks in melodramatic, absurd phrasing about her heritage—"I am every person who has lived here for nine hundred years. It's beyond ownership. It simply is" (88). She seems to sincerely believe that, although she is around 98 years old, her weapons cache, which includes boiling oil and swords, means she can fight off Howard (91). The Baroness also fills the role of the traditional Gothic villain, as she at first seduces Danny with some seemingly drugged wine and the supernatural ability to appear younger than she is. Danny first notices her in a tower as a young beautiful woman—a reference to the way the governess begins to be haunted in *The Turn of the Screw* by people who had previously lived in the Bly estate. Moreover, the Baroness locks everyone in the tunnels beneath the castle toward the end of the novel, live burials being, as Eve Sedgwick notes in her landmark work *The Coherence of Gothic Conventions* (1986), a particularly Gothic occurrence (20). The Baroness is also partly based on a real person; as mentioned in the introduction, while struggling to become a writer, Egan worked as the private secretary for a Countess, from 1988 to 1990 ("Countess"). Danny and the Countess represent reversals of traditional Gothic gender tropes; the things that happen to Danny usually happen to a female character, such as the governess and Mrs. Grose in *The Turn of the Screw,* or, more recently, the hauntings Sethe experiences in Toni Morrison's *Beloved* (1987). The Countess likewise represents a gender reversal, as the traditional Gothic villain is male, such as the evil and conniving Montoni in Ann Radcliffe's *The Mysteries of Udolpho.* Egan not only revels in the horror and the campiness of the Gothic, but toys with many of these conventions.

The Fantastic Nature of Digital Communication

Todorov defined the fantastic as a form of Gothic fiction that is "based essentially on a hesitation of the reader—a reader who identifies with the chief character—as to the nature of an uncanny event" (157). Through the multilayered narrative, the Gothic castle setting, and numerous strange events, *The Keep* is a text that provokes constant hesitations on the part of the reader. Hesitations are also built into the prose; as mentioned, Egan set herself the challenge of having a narrator who is learning how to write as the narrative progresses. Ray therefore makes some unusual structural choices, such as introducing speech in the form of a play script or using lists, and his writing sometimes fails to capture what he is trying to describe. This means the page is made up of literal pauses and hesitations: the reader pauses at each colon that introduces a speaker as the dialogue is formatted like a script. Hesitations are therefore evident in the prose style as well as in many events and happenings throughout the novel. Interestingly, Todorov queried in 1975, "why does the literature of the fantastic no longer exist?" (166). He claims the fantastic was a genre of the nineteenth century, for "the literature of the fantastic is nothing but the bad conscience of this positivist era" (168). Egan updates the fantastic to the contemporary—she, as I have noted before, both contemporizes the Gothic and Gothicizes the contemporary (Moran 230)—in order to explore the Gothic nature of digital communications, and to undercut the positivist understanding of technology that has dominated twenty-first century American life. The Gothic enables Egan to defamiliarize the supposed realness of the digital world, and to look at the staged authenticity at the heart of all digital communication.

In the opening scenes, Danny's invitation to the castle by his estranged cousin, Howard, is reminiscent of early moments in Poe's "The Fall of the House of Usher" (1839). As he tries to find his way into the castle, he experiences a series of hesitations. In an echo of how Phoebe sees King Ludwig's castle in *The Invisible Circus,* Danny is disconcerted when he has the sense that "he'd never been to a castle before or even this part of the world, but something about it all was familiar to Danny" (3). He wonders if he recognizes this castle "from a dream or a book," and "the towers had those square indentations around the top that little kids put on castles when they draw them" (3). Immediately, Egan signals that this will be a text full of hesitations, of characters not quite grasping or understanding what they are seeing. Once Danny has found his way into the castle, he hesitates as he tries to connect this adult "Howard" with the child "Howie" he knew: "The new Howie was fit. Built, even. Love handles, girly pear shape—gone. Liposuction? Exercise? Time passing? Who knew. On top of which he was tan. This part really threw Danny, because the old Howie had been white in a way that seemed deeper than not getting sun" (21). As well as echoing the doubles and doppelgangers of Gothic texts such as Poe's "William Wilson" (1839), the text begins with Danny hesitating and questioning whether this is the same Howie as before. Danny has rarely seen Howard since they were children, and not since the regrettable time that he and his other cousin, Rafe, left Howard for dead in the sewer tunnels under their hometown.[2] Howard, once a normal if nerdy child, was altered by this experience, a live burial that presages their later entombment by the Baroness. It is not until Danny notices an uneasiness reminiscent of the awkward *Dungeons and Dragons*–playing teenager he knew that he begins to see Howie in the man called Howard before him (36). Danny's struggle to recognize Howard immediately indicates that this a novel of the fantastic.

The hesitations extend beyond the characters in a manner that embodies the fantastic; Egan constantly builds up odd facts and images for the reader in *The Keep*. For instance, Danny believes he has "invisible skills": "He felt a prickling on the skin of his arms that gave him hope," as he thinks he can "feel on the surface of his skin when wireless internet access was available" (25). In contrast to his namesake Danny from *The Shining*, who definitively has supernatural powers, Egan leaves many such claims and happenings ambiguous, in order to create the fantastical experience of hesitation—in this instance, making the reader question whether this is possible or just hubris on Danny's part. To Charlie Reilly, Egan refers to this aspect of the Gothic she wishes the text to invoke: "one of the things that most interested me is that so often in Gothic novels the reader is left wondering what is really happening and what isn't." She suggests that "the reams of scholarly material" on *The Turn of the Screw* exist because it leaves this question open (443). Egan's insistence that no explanation should be given for these events places *The Keep* firmly in Todorov's definition of the fantastic in relation to its two neighboring genres, the marvelous and the uncanny: "If . . . the laws of reality remain intact and permit an explanation of the phenomena described, we say that the work belongs to another genre: the uncanny. If, on the contrary . . . new laws of nature must be entertained to account for the phenomena, we enter the genre of the marvelous" (41). An example of an uncanny novel would be Ann Radcliffe's *The Mysteries of*

Udolpho, where, as Egan complains to Josh Lukin, everything is eventually explained: "I think the mistake that she makes is that she provides a scientific explanation, which is really disappointing." A marvelous text would a text like *The Shining,* where the reader must accept the supernatural happenings King describes in The Overlook Hotel. As an instance of the fantastic, *The Keep* exists in this middle plane between the supernatural and the rational, leading both the characters and the reader to hesitate when deciding if these strange events are actually occurring.

The numerous narrative levels of *The Keep* work alongside the supernatural elements to create yet more hesitations for the reader, and so the metafictional elements work with, rather than against, the Gothic conventions of the text. Sherry R. Truffin (2013) discusses "Gothic metafiction," a tradition in which she mentions *The Keep* in passing (66), but it would be more accurate to call the novel's metafictional elements Gothic. Ray tells the reader: "I did make it up, I say, because I want Holly to think that. Otherwise it's all just stuff a guy told me, so why not be impressed with that guy instead of me?" (56). This admission raises the question of who is telling Ray the story, and near the end it is revealed that Ray believes the ghost of Danny is telling it to him from his cell window. After Danny is shot, the perspective shifts to Danny's consciousness in a form of purgatory; he follows the light, and at the end of the tunnel, he ends up at Ray's prison window: "It was a long walk, but when he finally got close to the door he realized it wasn't a door, it was a window. Danny couldn't see through it—the glass was foggy or dusty or maybe just warped. But when he got to the window and put his hand against it, the glass suddenly cleared . . . I saw him standing there. And he saw me" (221). The clichéd nature of the description does suggest that this is Ray's fictionalization, but the Gothic setting means the reader hesitates to dismiss Ray's version of events. The fantastic is situated within what Todorov labels "the duration of this uncertainty," and *The Keep* maintains this air of uncertainty throughout (25).

Hesitation also extends to Ray's level of the narrative. His cellmate, Davis, reveals that he has invented a contraption to speak with the dead, and while it may be "a shoebox full of dust with knobs pushed through the cardboard," Ray still hesitates to dismiss it as ridiculous: "what if it works? What if it actually does what Davis says?" (106). Ray hesitates, and "in that split second I go from pretending straight into believing—it's like pretending *made* me believe, except that doesn't make sense, because pretending and believing are opposites" (106). Considering he is already seeing a ghost, Ray hesitates to dismiss Davis as simply delusional. By struggling to conflate pretending and believing, Ray is having a distinctly fantastic experience, which Todorov defines as a moment when "the transition from mind to matter has become possible" (114).

Ray starts to believe this transition is possible, but again hesitates as he does so. From the nested structure, to the gender reversals of traditional Gothic tropes, to Danny's beliefs in his own special abilities, and Ray's experiences with Davis, *The Keep* constantly elicits hesitations from the reader.

These hesitations have a purpose; they are the tool by which Egan tries to defamiliarize and Gothicize contemporary digital communications. As she explained to Jennie Yabroff: "The questions had to do with telecommunications, and how it parallels supernatural experience. What does it mean that we are engaged in disembodied communication all day long?" In the same interview, she goes on to suggest the fine line between a person speaking to themselves and speaking into their mobile phone: "And they may actually be in la-la land, in which case they actually are hearing voices and responding to them. Gee, that's an awful lot like being on the phone. At a certain point, what's the difference?" Danny has lugged a satellite dish across Eastern Europe to wherever they are, desperate to stay connected while he is away from New York.[3] While still trying to work out how to enter the castle, "Danny took out his cell phone and flipped it open. He didn't have international service, but the phone lit up, searching, and just seeing it do that calmed Danny down, like the phone had power" (11). This power operates "like it was a Forcefield Stabilizer left over from Terminal Zeus" (11). That this connectedness is compared with a childhood game of Danny's alludes to its illusory nature; the fantastical, hesitation-inducing nature of the Gothic setting enables Egan to equate contemporary technology with the imaginary and the seemingly supernatural.

Danny cannot get a signal, so he finds a tower in the castle where he hopes he can make his satellite dish work. His notion of connectedness via the internet is a fantastical understanding of turning mind into matter: "All he knew was that he lived more or less in a constant state of expecting something any day, any hour, that would change everything, knock the world upside down and put Danny's whole life into perspective as a story of complete success" (69). But Danny's satellite dish falls into a pool, leaving him cut off from his connections: "Nope. It was dead, and not that tunnelly deadness of an open line—that would've been the sound of angels singing in heaven compared to this, which was the sound of no sound—an object that was just *what it was* didn't lead to anything or anyplace or anyone" (75). That he compares the sound of an open line to "angels" points to the almost religious faith Danny has in these devices. At the start of the novel, his belief in his need for these connections is emphasized to the point of absurdity: "His brain refused to stay locked up inside the echo chamber of his head—it spilled out, it overflowed and poured across the world until it was touching a thousand people who had nothing to do with him . . . if Danny kept it locked up inside his skull, a pressure began to build" (12).

Danny's need to stay connected has become a psychological crutch, and losing that connection leads him to act strangely and distrust what he sees and hears. However, Danny's desire for information leads him to lean too far out of the window of the keep while listening to Mick and Ann speak of their affair. The severe brain trauma Danny suffers due to his fall means his seemingly supernatural experiences could be a result of this injury, and so once again hesitation is built into how we interpret the events Danny experiences.

The contrast between Danny's beliefs in his technology and Howard's plans for his hotel is another means by which Egan depicts digital communication as consisting of fantastical hesitations. In a long discussion, Howard explains to Danny that he sees contemporary communications as illusory, and as detrimental to a very loosely defined "real" experience. Howard claims, "The machines are so small now, and using them is so easy—we're a half step away from telepathy," and Danny immediately undercuts him: '"Except we're talking to people who are *there*. You can hear them" (135). Howard is insistent on the fact that '"They're not *there,* Danny. Where's there? You have no idea where they are . . . No one's ever there, Danny. You're alone. That's the reality" (135–136). Howard insists it is impossible to be certain that whoever is speaking is real, and that Danny has an unspoken *faith* that this digital reality is as it seems. Danny also fails to question his own fallibility when using technology, such as when he is looking for the castle online: "Danny couldn't even find it online, although he hadn't been sure about the spelling" (4). Egan here points to another important pitfall of using technology; it functions only as well as the user knows how to use it—it is a tool made active by the user, as Danny finds out with his satellite dish once it falls into the pool. Howard asserts to Danny that digital communication systems are fantastic, and in doing so points to an underlying assumption in every usage of modern technology: "What's real, Danny? Is reality TV real? Are confessions you read on the Internet real? The words are real, *someone* wrote them, but beyond that the question doesn't even make sense. Who are you talking to on your cell phone? In the end you have no fucking idea" (137). Here, Howard almost directly rebukes the "authenticity" that Thomas Keene believed he was depicting in *Look at Me*. It is on these grounds that Howard insists, "We're living in a supernatural world, Danny. We're surrounded by ghosts" (137). By creating Gothic hesitations in this ubiquitous aspect of contemporary experience, Egan's novel, as I have discussed before, resembles Alan Kirby's arguments in *Digimodernism* (Moran 232). For Kirby, "Web 2.0 depends so critically on the apparently real that it gives a name ('trolls') to those who reject it" (142). Through the Gothic hesitations of the subgenre of the fantastic, *The Keep* suggests digital communication becomes another instance of staged authenticity; Danny is invested in these communications being real, rather than a digital stage in which people project their best selves.

Kirby goes on to proclaim that sincerity is demanded of each interaction in the digital world, and this discussion of sincerity relates to the debates around Adam Kelly's concept of New Sincerity, which builds largely from his reading of David Foster Wallace's texts (and specifically *Infinite Jest*). However, Lee Konstantinou persuasively points out that there is essentially an a priori belief in the possibility of sincerity built into Kelly's formulations: "Postironic belief must precede the ethics of New Sincerity" (175). Similarly, Howard reveals to Danny that an unspoken faith undergirds his usage of technology. Kirby puts this idea of sincerity in a wider contemporary context: "While sincerity is a value, a conscious moral choice reassuringly (in troubled times) under the control and will of a speaker, digimodernist earnestness, like postmodern irony, has deep roots in contemporary culture. It can therefore seem a compulsive mode, involuntarily swamping its speaker" (151). Danny perfectly embodies being "swamped" by "digimodernist earnestness" in how he interacts; he even sees death in the loss of communication possibilities: "That's what death is, Danny thought: wanting to talk to someone and not being able to" (82). Egan indicates that fantastical assumptions are needed to conceive of these connections as more than a staged version of authenticity. While in *Look at Me* claims of authenticity or sincerity are shown to be ethically questionable, in *The Keep* sincerity becomes a ghostly presumption, a fantastical belief essential for all online interaction.

What happens when this belief collapses is shown when Danny gets through to his girlfriend Martha in New York using Mick's phone. Danny is immediately skeptical it is her, so he asks for "some identifying information" (176). The bad connection, his strange line of questioning, and the fact that Danny was in trouble when he left New York combine to make Martha suspicious about whom she is speaking to. For both parties, the veracity of this call collapses: Martha states, "I don't believe you're Danny," to which Danny replies: "I don't believe you're Martha" (176). This theme of miscommunication through technology also connects *The Keep* to previous Gothic novels, which often feature moments of miscommunication and misreadings that lead to violence and tragedy. In Walpole's *The Castle of Otranto,* Manfred stabs his own daughter, Matilda, mistaking her for Isabella; in Radcliffe's *The Mysteries of Udolpho,* Emily misreads the blood on the steps of the castle as belonging to her Aunt, Madame Cheron, and therefore mistakenly believes she is dead. This theme continues in neo-Gothic novels like Toni Morrison's *Beloved,* where Sethe misinterprets the intentions of the helpful white man and tries to attack him with an ice pick. And in *The Shining,* Jack and Wendy both think they have hurt Danny toward the end of the text. Similarly, after they escape from the keep, Danny tries to stab Ray. Danny's whole world is communication and information; when he begins to hesitate to trust this, he turns on Ray. Meanwhile, Ray is suspicious of Danny, questions his motives, and responds to Danny's attack by shooting him. This misunderstanding results in a particularly Gothic death for Danny, shot through the head by Ray, the result of fantastical events that make him hesitate and misinterpret the world around him. But in contrast to many of these other Gothic deaths, Danny's death is in relation to the collapse of his trust in digital communication; for instance, in his call to Martha, he begins to doubt whether the conversation is a stage, and he is actually speaking with someone else. Consequently, through the fantastical world of the Gothic, Egan shows the staged authenticity of every online interaction—and once Danny begins to see the possibility that the authenticity of these connections is questionable, his identity, based on permanent connectivity, falls apart.

Staged Authenticity and Howard's Hotel

Howard's purchase of the castle is a means for him to theorize about contemporary entertainment, and to voice his sincere belief in the need to reinvigorate everyone's imaginations. In many ways, Howard believes he is the remedy to the sort of reality that Thomas Keene helps create in *Look at Me*. By building a hotel as a reaction to this situation, Howard once again represents the manner in which instances of staged authenticity—in this case, online life—lead to the creation of something that purports to reveal the backstage of that world. He says, "think about medieval times, Danny, like when this castle was built. People were constantly seeing ghosts, having visions" (47). Howard believes we have lost touch with some deeper, inner experience: "Was all that stuff happening before and then it stopped? Unlikely. Was everyone nuts in medieval times? Doubtful. But their *imaginations* were more active. Their inner lives were rich and weird" (47). Howard squarely blames contemporary entertainment for this lack of creativity: "We've lost the ability to make things up. We've farmed out that job to the entertainment industry, and we sit around and drool on ourselves while they do it for us" (48). To put Howard's proclamations in the language of the fantastic, he wants to embrace the possibilities of a transition from mind to matter, and to suggest the Gothic nature of contemporary communications technology. He is yet another character in Egan's fiction who believes he has some access to a pure sense of authenticity, that he can reach beyond the velvet ropes and access the true core of reality. Moreover, as his hotel is designed specifically for tourists, it connects directly with MacCannell's initial definitions of the concept: a managed area designed for visitors to experience a tightly controlled image of authenticity.

Howard seeks to recreate a lost sense of authenticity, an imaginary realm that is distinct from the entertainment industry. His nostalgia for some sort of lost past links him to Robert McLaughlin's description of the post-postmodern era as one where writers attempt to "reconnect" with "something real" (213). However, Egan shows in *The Keep* that this "something real" also follows distinct conventions and requires certain limits in order to function. When he and Danny discover the tunnels to the castle, Howard makes a speech that outlines his "mission": "The whole mission of this hotel we're putting together is to help people shed the real/unreal binary that's become so meaningless now, with telecommunications" (197–198). Earlier in the text, Howard outlines another mission: "My *mission* is to bring some of that back. Let people be tourists of their own imaginations. And please don't say *like Disneyland,* because that's the exact opposite of what I'm talking about" (48). While Howard's big idea is to build a hotel free from commercial demands, it is precisely a commercial demand he is filling by offering such a retreat. Once again, the reader hesitates to accept these proclamations; the project for the hotel is itself an image of the fantastic.

Even in describing his project, Howard slips into the language of branding, such as when he describes to Danny his concept of "The Imagination Pool." Incidentally, this is the pool in which Danny loses his satellite dish, and which definitively activates his imagination, as it is here he sees the ghosts of the Von Ausblinker twins (another nod to King's *The Shining,* as well as another instance of twins in Egan's fiction). Howard describes this as a place where "you dive in and—*bang*—your imagination is released: it's yours again, not Hollywood's, not the networks or Lifetime TV or *Vanity Fair* or whatever crap video game you're addicted to. *You* make it up, *you* tell the story, and then you're free. You can do anything you want" (50). Danny is suspicious of Howard's motives, and Howard also concedes when Danny questions if people will pay for this experience, that this is "the only question, from a business standpoint" (48). Howard's hotel is caught in the paradox of wishing to escape from commercial needs while fulfilling a commercialized need for escape. In this sense, Howard's Gothic hotel works as a synecdoche for Egan's use of genre. As Nicholas Brown posits regarding the use of popular genres by numerous writers of contemporary fiction, the very artifice of genre forms "opens up a zone of autonomy within the heteronomous space of cultural commodities, allowing the commodity character to be addressed as an aspect of the material support" (26). It is within these borders that Howard is able to respond to the demands of the market, and also to sell visitors the promise of a space somehow separate from it. Similarly, Egan's use of the Gothic enables her to write both a genre novel and one that plays with this form. Again, *The Keep,* as a novel of the fantastic, finds itself in an unsettling middle ground, unable to be defined as a genre novel or a literary novel. Similarly, Howard's hotel is simultaneously a retreat that many visitors find valuable and a commercial enterprise that seeks to extract as much capital from its visitors as possible.

The value of the evident artifice of genre forms is displayed in the final section, which switches to the perspective of Holly, Ray's writing instructor. After Danny has died and Ray has escaped from prison, Holly is questioned about Ray's escape by the police. Ray has mailed her the manuscript of the novel we have supposedly been reading, and she fears the police can tell she has buried the text, much like the narrator in Poe's "The Tell-Tale Heart" (1843). After the ordeal of being mistakenly arrested, she decides to visit the castle herself. Holly is amazed at the exorbitant cost of her trip, which emphasizes this is a business venture for Howard: "I didn't think a hotel could be so expensive—to pay for two nights plus airfare, I have to cash in part of my 401K" (244). Before leaving, she receives an envelope from Howard's hotel, scented with vanilla and spice, containing a note that dramatically proclaims she is "on the verge of an experience that will send you home a slightly different person than the one you are right now." This note leads Holly to "laugh out loud," once again suggesting the cheesy, earnest campiness of the Gothic mode (246). The letter emphasizes that other than "live medieval music at dinnertime" the details of the rest of her stay are supposedly up to her (246). However, everything is actually tightly controlled, and what Holly gets to experience is a staged form of authenticity. When she gets to her room, there is a note that reads, "Our premises are secure. You may go wherever you wish, day or night. . . . Our staff is plentiful and, we hope, unobtrusive" (249). But these limits do not undercut any experience Holly has in the castle; in fact, they are generative of a redemptive ending for her. At the very end of the novel, she stands at the edge of Howard's Imagination Pool, and experiences a sense of "childish excitement" (255). She then dives in, reemerges (with obvious religious echoes), and cries by the pool, despite her earlier pronouncement that she is "dry" of tears after the stillbirth of her son (225).

Interestingly, this entire scene is foreshadowed earlier in the novel by Ann, Howard's wife, when she describes her vision of how the pool will work for guests: "A woman travels here by herself. She's unhappy, she's—shut down. Maybe her marriage is in trouble; maybe she's alone. Whatever it is, she's become numb, dead to herself. So she checks in and leaves her stuff in her room and then she comes through the garden to this pool . . . it *does* something to her. Being in that water does something: it wakes her up. And when she gets back out of the pool, she feels strong again. Like she's ready to start her life over" (49–50). As well as suggesting that Holly may have edited the text of

Ray's novel to describe her final experiences, the fact that Ann's vision happens so exactly is suggestive of how the limits of genres work; this management of limits is generative of a specific experience for Holly, as well as for the reader. Lee Konstantinou sees a similar process at work in *A Visit from The Goon Squad*: "Egan means to show, in the final chapters of her popular novel, that reified forms (such as PowerPoint) allow for genuine artistic expression and emotional involvement for her characters, and, by allegorical extension, for the contemporary novelist" (43). Egan therefore suggests the Gothic nature of modern communications technology, and the need to believe in this staged authenticity for it to function. However, staged authenticity is also shown to have redemptive value, and the tensions, hesitations, and compromises inherent in such experiences do not completely erase their value. The tension between artistic purity and commercial demands continues to be explored in the polyphonic and multi-award winning *A Visit from the Goon Squad,* a text which in many ways summarizes everything Egan has explored from *Emerald City* to *The Keep.*

6

A Visit from the Goon Squad

Buoyed by numerous awards and a relentless promotional tour, *A Visit from the Goon Squad* launched Egan to a new level of popularity. The book won the Pulitzer Prize and National Book Critics Circle Award, beating Jonathan Franzen's *Freedom* (2010) to both prizes. In 2019, *Entertainment Weekly* dubbed it the best work of fiction of the decade ("Here Are"), while the *Guardian* selected it as the twenty-fourth best work of fiction of the twenty-first century ("The 100 Best"). It was optioned for an HBO series (which never materialized), and Egan became an in-demand writer, being interviewed by the *New Yorker, Wall Street Journal, Guardian,* and the BBC, and she was invited to give a talk at Google (Itzkoff). *Goon Squad* has been integrated into numerous contemporary fiction courses, and more articles, chapters, and references to this text exist than to all of her other work put together. After years of her fiction being treated as a byword for excellence rather than analysis, *Goon Squad* has placed Egan, not beside literary trends, but at the center of many debates and discussions; its themes of punk music, time, aging, and authenticity are analyzed by a wide array of critics. Neither a novel nor a collection but rather something in-between, there is much debate over how to define and categorize the text. There is also some conjecture over when exactly everything takes place. To help readers navigate this sprawling yet tightly controlled work, I begin by outlining its long genesis. I then provide a table to unravel the text's byzantine structure. The majority of the chapter explores the central themes, which once again center on authenticity. Moreover, I suggest throughout this chapter that with *Goon Squad* Egan revisits many of the preoccupations she has shown in her work to date, particularly the effects of technological connectivity and surveillance on contemporary experience.

Goon Squad is made up of thirteen chapters, each of which operates as an independent short story. The fourth chapter, "Safari," is set in 1973, and is thus the novel's earliest episode chronologically. The latest, "Pure Language," is set in the early 2020s and forms the book's final chapter. The central chapter, "A to B," is the only chapter that remains in place when the others are moved into chronological order. There is also "Black Box," a story Egan released via the *New Yorker* Twitter account in 2012, which takes the character Lulu from *Goon Squad* and follows her as a cyborg spy about a decade after the events of "Pure Language." The out-of-sequence timeline is arranged to mirror the sides of a vinyl record, as the text has an A side and a B side. This structure pays homage to the concept album and captures one of the novel's central themes: the winnowing of the album format due to the shift to digital music. Readers follow two main characters, Bennie Salazar and Sasha Grady (later, Sasha Blake). Bennie was born in 1962, the same year as Egan, and attended high school in San Francisco, just like Egan, and she clearly mines her teenage years here for these scenes. Bennie was a teen punk in late 1970s and early 1980s San Francisco, and he was part of a band called the Flaming Dildos. He becomes a highly successful record producer in New York after discovering a band called the Conduits who embody the "late-eighties sound somewhere between punk and ska" (125). Bennie then sells his label, Sow's Ear Records, and moves to Crandale, New York, to live among the elite. Here, he cheats on his wife, Stephanie, with a woman from their country club. The first time the reader meets him in the text is in the second chapter, a year and half after his divorce, eating gold flakes as an aphrodisiac. In the final chapter, he is promoting a free concert by his high school friend, Scotty Hausmann, in a dystopian New York, a city marked by the effects of climate change and "two generations of war and surveillance" (335).

Then there is Sasha, born in 1972. We follow her from a troubled early life, which involves a trip to Asia to follow a drummer from a band called the Pin Heads, and then to Naples, a route that echoes Egan's own travels as well as Phoebe and Faith's experiences in *The Invisible Circus*. After being brought home by her art historian uncle Ted Hollander, we meet Sasha again in her college years. There is a brief glimpse of her in the chapter "A to B" near the start of her twelve years as Bennie's assistant. She is fired by Bennie for having "sticky fingers," a phrase which, as well as nodding to *The Rolling Stones* album of the same name, refers to Sasha's compulsive stealing (338). The next event is the chapter that begins the text, "Found Objects," where Sasha is a thirty-five-year-old kleptomaniac who steals a purse while on a date with a man, Alex, she met online. Finally, in the penultimate chapter, "Great Rock and

Roll Pauses"—famously written in PowerPoint slides—we see Sasha happily married to her college boyfriend, Drew, with two children and living in the California desert sometime in the 2020s. This chapter depicts a fuller picture of the dystopian world shown in Bennie's final section, as the destructive effects of climate change mean a new currency of "credits" is now needed in order to have a lawn, and the desert is covered in solar panels which are "mending the earth" (291). Sasha has turned her need to steal into a form of art using found objects that she displays in the desert, echoing the art of Klara Sax in DeLillo's *Underworld* (1997). The future shown at the end of Sasha's storyline is one of repair and redemption, for both herself and the world around her.

On the next page begins a table in which I reorder the chapters into chronological order, based on small snippets of information that Egan provides in the text. The earliest scenes are, as mentioned, in 1973, and the narrative concludes sometime in 2032 with "Black Box." Most chapters take place within a single year, but for "A to B" and "Selling the General" I provide the range of years in which these events take place. I note the position in the text of each section, and whether it is in first-, second-, or third-person perspective. I also note the year in which I believe it is set, providing evidence for this claim in the final column. My years differ slightly from David Cowart's chronology, as there are a couple of details he has overlooked (233). Finally, critics have offered some definitive dates when the chapters "Great Rock and Roll Pauses" and "Pure Language" take place—for instance, John Masterson argues that this chapter is set as late as 2025 (70)—but I do not believe this date can be definitively ascertained. Moreover, it is possible that "Great Rock and Roll Pauses" is chronologically the final chapter; the reader has no real way to confirm the order of these two chapters, so distinct are the events contained in each.

Influences

Influenced by both *The Sopranos* and Marcel Proust in equal measure, Egan zooms in and out on different characters connected to Bennie and Sasha, never settling on one point of view for more than a chapter (Kachka). As shown in the table outlining the chapters, there are five chapters told in the first person, two told in the second person, and seven in the third person. *Goon Squad* is, in David Cowart's phrase, "a downsized, epistemically chastened Proust for the twenty-first century" (180). To take one example of this connection, in the first volume of Proust's epic musings the narrator notes his family had a quarrel with his uncle Adolphe. The petty cause of this breach is the narrator's failure to raise his hat to his uncle: "My uncle thought that in doing this I was following my parents' orders, he did not forgive them, and he died many years later without any of us ever seeing him again" (81–82). Lou, Bennie's mentor, has a son named

YEAR SET, CHAPTER TITLE (POSITION IN TEXT), POINT OF VIEW	SUMMARY	EVIDENCE
1973 Safari (4) 3rd person	Lou and Mindy on Safari in Kenya with Lou's children, Rolph and Charlie.	"Thirty-five years from now, in 2008, this warrior will be caught in the tribal violence between the Kikuyu and the Luo and will die in a fire" (61).
1979 Ask Me if I Care (3) 1st person, Rhea	Rhea, Jocelyn, Alice, Bennie, Scotty perform at the Mab in San Francisco; Lou begins relationship with Jocelyn.	"Nineteen eighty is almost here" (40). Jocelyn is 17 here, so born 1962, same as Egan. Meets Lou hitchhiking (42, 87). Hitchhiking pickup happened "weeks ago" (42) confirming it was 1979 when Lou and Jocelyn met.
1991 Goodbye, My Love (11) 3rd person	Ted Hollander, Sasha's uncle, goes to Naples to bring her home after she has run away for 2 years.	"Sasha disappeared two years ago, at seventeen" (213), so 19 here, and "almost 21" in "Out of Body." More than 20 years later, Ted visits Sasha, Drew, and their children at home in desert. This suggests "Great Rock and Roll Pauses" set somewhere between 2012 and 2020 (233).
1993 Out of Body (10) 2nd person	Rob, Sasha's closeted college friend, dies drowning while high on ecstasy, attempting to swim in river with Drew, Sasha's college boyfriend and future husband.	Sasha and Drew took greyhound to DC to see Bill Clinton inauguration while Rob in Tampa, so situates this as early 1993 (192). Sasha "almost 21" (192).

YEAR SET, CHAPTER TITLE (POSITION IN TEXT), POINT OF VIEW	SUMMARY	EVIDENCE
1997 X's and O's (6) 1st person, Scotty	Scotty, post-divorce from Alice, lives in small apartment. He fishes in the Hudson, and visits Bennie in his huge office, giving him a fish.	Chris is 3 months old (102). He is 9 in "The Gold Cure," so this chapter is 9 years before that chapter.
2000 article, 1999 attack Forty-Minute Lunch (9) 1st person article, Jules Jones	Newspaper article from Jules Jones, Bennie's brother-in-law, about his attempted rape of Kitty Jackson, a global film star.	Writing 1 year after arrest, so 2 years after Kitty's movie *Oh, Baby, Oh* (170). She is 28 in "Selling the General," and film released 10 years before that, so she is 18 here (144).
2001–2004 A to B (7) 3rd person	Bennie lives in Crandale, New York, with his wife, Stephanie, and they join a country club. Stephanie gets into tennis, Jules is released from prison and lives with them, and he agrees to write book about Bosco's final tour. Stephanie discovers Bennie is having an affair at the end of the section.	Chris is in kindergarten (112), so 5 or 6 years old. Takes from winter to June to get membership to country club (111). "He'd sold his record label last year" (113). Chris now in first grade (115). Jules in prison 5 years (119), so situates his release as 5 years after attack in 1999. Bennie is 42 (123).
2006 You (Plural) (5) 1st person, Jocelyn	Lou is dying; Bennie brings everyone back together to say goodbye. Jocelyn, now clean and sober, struggles when comparing her life to her friends from her youth.	At least 3 months before "The Gold Cure," as Bennie notes he was with Lou when he died in that chapter (37). Rhea and Jocelyn are 43 (86), so 26 years after they were 17 near end of 1979.

2006 Gold Cure (2) 3rd person	Bennie is eating gold flakes as aphrodisiac. He takes his son, Chris, to see one of his bands, Stop/Go, with Sasha. Tries to kiss Sasha; she turns him down.	Bennie is 44 (21). Sold label 5 years previously (23). Chris is 9 (24). A year and half since he and Stephanie broke up (26). Sasha at NYU when first met at Conduits gig, puts her in her 30s (28). Lou dead 3 months earlier (37).
2007 Found Objects (1) 3rd person	Sasha is on date with Alex, steals a purse which she then returns. Sasha and Alex have sex at Sasha's apartment.	Bennie no longer Sasha's boss, so after "The Gold Cure" (5). Sasha is 35. 21 in 1993, so year is 2007 (6).
2008–2009 Selling the General (8) 3rd person	Dolly "La Doll" is hired by Arc to change public image of a genocidal dictator of unnamed country. Dolly then visits the general to implement her scheme of getting him a girlfriend, Kitty Jackson, the famous actress from before. She speaks out of turn, is taken hostage, but the relentlessness of the paparazzi somehow leads the country to democracy. Dolly moves upstate in final scenes, and Arc, the general's advisor, visits her in America.	La Doll's Oil party 2 years previously (141), on New Year's Eve. Bennie has scars from the "recent debacle" in 2006 in "The Gold Cure" (22). Kitty is 28 (144). Kitty's famous film *Oh Baby Oh* 10 years earlier, and Jules notes she was 18 in "Forty Minute-Lunch" when that was released (144). A year later is Jules's attack (144). Lulu is 9 (146). Arc and Dolly speak "almost" a year later (163).
Early 2020s Great Rock and Roll Pauses (12) 1st person, Allison	Possibly later than final chapter. Sasha and Drew now married, live in California desert with Allison, their 12-year-old daughter, and Lincoln, their autistic son. Lincoln obsessed with pauses in music. Allison makes PowerPoint journals. Dystopian future.	Alison is 12, and her brother, Lincoln, is 13 (236).

YEAR SET, CHAPTER TITLE (POSITION IN TEXT), POINT OF VIEW	SUMMARY	EVIDENCE
Winter early 2020s, no earlier than 2022 Pure Language (13) 3rd person	Bennie hires Alex to clandestinely promote a concert by Scotty. Alex works with Lulu, daughter of Dolly, to promote concert. New York ravaged by climate change, war, and surveillance, and section ends with Scotty's concert, which is a huge success.	Bennie "pushing sixty" (312). Lulu in "early twenties" (317). Concert is in January (322). Scotty's fish visit in "X's and O's" chapter was "twenty-some-odd-years ago" (333). "The weight of what had happened here more than twenty years ago was still faintly present for Alex, as it always was when he came to the Footprint" (331), so at least 2022, as "more than" 20 years since 9/11.
Early 2032 Black Box (14) 2nd person, Lulu	Lulu has volunteered to be a cyborg infiltrating a "designated mate," with her body as a receptacle of any information she acquires. Gets shot in escape; final moment is her bleeding in a boat, waiting to be rescued.	Lulu thinks: "You will reflect on the fact that you are thirty-three, and have spent your professional life fomenting musical trends" ("Black Box"). 9 years old in "Selling the General," so set 24 years after that.

Rolph, and during a safari trip to Kenya in 1973, the narrator reaches forward in time to see that Rolph's sister, Charlie, will return to this memory of Rolph dancing "again and again, for the rest of her life, long after Rolph has shot himself in the head in their father's house at twenty-eight" (82). Moments of prolepsis are repeated throughout *Goon Squad*, and particularly in "Safari." For example, the narrator explains that "thirty-five years from now, in 2008," one of the dancers "will be caught in the tribal violence between the Kikuyu and the Luo and will die in a fire" (61). His grandson will then move to New York and marry Lulu, "where he'll invent a scanning device that becomes standard issue for crowd security" (62). These devices are evident in the final chapter, a section which features Bennie talking about his future with Alex proleptically: "we have some history together that hasn't happened yet" (311). In crisscrossing back and forth through time, Egan creates a mosaic of these lives, with the gaps in the story as noticeable as the events that are told. Indeed, many of the most consequential actions occur off the page.

For instance, Sasha's wealthy stepfather, who pays for her uncle to go to Naples and pulls strings to get Sasha, a high school dropout, into NYU, is left off the page. We only see Sasha's birth father, Andy Grady, in glimpses, and Sasha warns her therapist away from discussing him because "in that direction lay only sorrow" (9). Sasha's dramatic trip to reunite with Drew in Pakistan, marry him, and have two children, is also only briefly mentioned. Beyond Sasha, each character has dramatic events left off the page. Jocelyn, one of Bennie's high school friends and girlfriend of the much older Lou, is known to have seen her father with the "leather boys" at a San Francisco gay club, the White Swallow, before his death due to AIDS, but this information is only glanced at (43). Jocelyn's relationship with Lou is also only seen in retrospect, when she visits Lou on his deathbed when she is forty-three, and Lou is in his late sixties. The global catastrophes that have created the conditions for the dystopian world of the last two chapters are left largely unrepresented, or only hinted at. Repeatedly in *Goon Squad,* we see characters after they have experienced dramatic events, but the drama is left off the page for the reader to fill in. Through its proleptic, tangled structure, the gaps and pauses contain much of the drama. In this regard, the PowerPoint chapter, "Great Rock and Roll Pauses," works as a synecdoche for the entire novel, where gaps, pauses, and strict formatting rules define each slide.

As a result of its unusual form, *Goon Squad* is often discussed as either an example of, or a development out of, experimental postmodern literature. Martin Moling asserts that the PowerPoint chapter in particular "exhibits [Egan's] postmodern experimentation with new and eclectic forms of writing" (53). Conversely, in his review for *The Washington Post,* Ron Charles lauds *Goon*

Squad as leaving postmodern experiments behind, situating the text as "our reward for living through the self-conscious gimmicks and ironic claptrap of postmodernism." One could connect some moments to postmodern classics—for example, the fact that Bennie's therapist is named Dr. Beet, the musical pun being clear, is reminiscent of Thomas Pynchon's Dr. Hilarius from *The Crying of Lot 49* (1965), in that both names represent what Martin Paul Eve labels in Egan's fiction more broadly "her postmodern urge toward nominative determinism" ("Textual" 30). However, as discussed in the introduction, for Egan such claims dehistoricize the novel. In her words, "Look at a book like *Tristram Shandy,* which is so crazily experimental in a way we still have yet to match," and, "How about Cervantes? How crazy is *Don Quixote*?" (Michod). And Eve's claim that punning names is somehow postmodern ignores that this is perhaps another feature over which postmodern writers like Pynchon cannot completely claim ownership. Egan expands her point beyond Cervantes and Sterne to assert, "Even nineteenth-century novels [she is referring particularly to George Eliot's *Middlemarch*], which are supposed to be so staid, they're actually not" (Michod). Dickens is one such nineteenth-century figure who particularly toys with aptronyms, such as Ebenezer Scrooge in *A Christmas Carol* (1843). Egan situates *Goon Squad* not as a postmodern or a post-postmodern text, but one that continues to experiment with fictional forms in a way that hearkens back to texts produced long before postmodernism.

Placed in the traditions of Cervantes and Sterne, *Goon Squad* can comfortably be understood as a novel, and numerous critics have defined it as such. Caroline Edwards reads it as a "network novel" (220), and David Watson labels it a "multi-stranded novel" (90). However, this is not definitive; *Goon Squad* can also be situated as part of the longer literary tradition of the short story cycle. As Jennifer Smith describes it, this genre includes Sherwood Anderson's *Winesburg, Ohio* (1919), Ernest Hemingway's *In Our Time* (1925), and William Faulkner's *Knights Gambit* (1949). Moreover, "the genre proliferates in moments of communal or national change, such as industrialisation, war, or decolonization" (Smith 5). In the case of *Goon Squad,* Egan charts a transition to the digital world, which she similarly explored in *Look at Me* and *The Keep.* However, while persuasive, this classification is again not definitive, as *Goon Squad* began life as a story collection, and it is fair to see it as such. The chapter "X's and O's" was published in *GQ* in 1998, and "Forty-Minute Lunch" first appeared in a 1999 edition of *Harper's,* and is largely unchanged in the final text.[1] In 2001 she was already discussing the title, and notably referring to it as a collection: "I've had a collection in mind for a while, called *A Visit from the Goon Squad,* and I've already written some stories for that" (Hogan). Indeed, nine of the thirteen chapters were to appear as separate stories from 1998 to

2010, and some have been included in collections after the publication of *Goon Squad*.[2] Writing a series of standalone stories has undoubtedly been lucrative, and the ability to spin off and write more stories set in this world, such as "Black Box," has also worked well for Egan.[3] *Goon Squad* can therefore be discussed as a novel, a short story cycle, or a collection; it is betwixt and between these fictional forms, part of several traditions rather than representing just one.

The form of *Goon Squad* took a long time to take shape, and Egan often referred to it by name as a "collection" she was writing. That all changed when Egan read Kate Walbert's similarly structured novel, *Our Kind*. In her 2004 review of *Our Kind*, Egan says, "I have never been a huge fan of what are sometimes known as 'related short stories'—collections whose tales draw on a common world and set of characters" ("Reader"). Egan describes such collections as "the spawn of writing programs," the product of a workshop environment that "favors shorter projects" ("Reader"). One example would be the second half of Michael Chabon's collection *A Model World and Other Stories* (1991), which follows the Shapiro family, leaping forward in time with each story. In describing these collections in such terms Egan once again shows her distance from the aesthetic standards encouraged by university writing programs, the context in which Chabon wrote many of his stories for *A Model World*. Moreover, in the aforementioned 2001 interview, she says, "For me, stories are always something I slip into between other things," so she clearly saw the novel as a more challenging and rewarding form of writing (Hogan). She makes this feeling explicit in the review of *Our Kind*, where she confesses that "these hybrids have struck me in the past as trying to have the impact of novels without actually doing the work of novels" ("Reader"). However, Egan proclaims that "Kate Walbert has changed my mind about this." Walbert's *Our Kind*, which follows a series of characters who are older and are looking back at their lives, is a similarly proleptic work that follows a community of people in upstate New York. Egan states that until she read Walbert's text she did not know "how fascinated by time" she was—and continues to be (Lukin). While there are elements of this in *Goon Squad*, and the theme of nostalgia is prominent, Egan experiments with form and perspective in a way that Walbert does not. Nonetheless, Walbert's text is a clear influence on the final form that *Goon Squad* took.

For each chapter, Egan set herself three rules: "1) Each chapter had to be about a different person. 2) Each chapter had to have a different mood and tone and approach. 3) Each chapter had to stand completely on its own" ("Reader's Guide"). This structure was partly inspired by the art of Brice Marden, an abstract expressionist who similarly sets himself arbitrary rules for each piece and then follows them through to the end. In Egan's notes attached to an auctioned first edition, she explains how she saw the structure of *Goon Squad* as a "tangle" that resembles Marden's art, which is often marked by strings of color mixed together (Christie's). Moreover, Egan has stated that she considers these stories less linked than "entangled," further accentuating the connection to Marden's work (Ciabattari). Mirroring the form of the text, Egan also drew from a jumble of influences. As well as Proust and *The Sopranos,* Egan later realized how much she had been influenced by Quentin Tarantino's *Pulp Fiction* (1994): "I was just *copying* this movie! I even have a character named Jules! Oh my God. In a way, it's slightly frightening. I mean, how much was I really influenced?" (La Force). There is another possible connection in the chapter called "The Gold Cure," as it has a remarkably similar name to the chapter of *Pulp Fiction* called "The Gold Solution." Through these conscious and unconscious borrowings—*The Sopranos, Pulp Fiction,* Brice Marden, Proust, DeLillo, and Kate Walbert—Egan created a richly original work of fiction.

The tangled structure of *Goon Squad* is also representative of how connections are made online, and the tangled web of interactions and memories that are stored on social media in particular. Developing the surveillance and connectivity themes of her journalism, *Look at Me,* and *The Keep,* numerous characters in *Goon Squad* are only connected, or reconnected, through the internet. This fact is introduced in the first chapter, as Alex and Sasha plan their date via an online app. Moreover, Sasha has lied about her age to Alex; she is 35, and even her therapist, Coz, does not know her real age; "Her online profiles all listed her as twenty-eight" (6). That Sasha is lying about her age echoes Charlotte's similar falsehoods in *Look at Me* and continues Egan's exploration of how people manage their identities, particularly in online discourse, something she delves into in her journalism as well as *The Keep.* The chapter "You (Plural)," in which Bennie has brought all of his school friends back together to say goodbye to the dying Lou, is made possible by the internet. As Jocelyn, the narrator of this short chapter, realizes, "It seems you [can] find almost anyone on a computer" (84–85). Similarly, Sasha is able to find her college boyfriend, Drew, on Facebook, leading them to reconnect, marry, and have two children (233). Indeed, even in the earlier chapter, "Safari," set in 1973, a shared experience in which one of the visitors is attacked by a lion which is then killed by their guide, Albert, becomes a motive to reconnect in the future: "It will prompt some of them, years from now, to search for each other on Google and Facebook, unable to resist the wish-fulfilment fantasy these portals offer" (71). Here, connectivity is linked to the Freudian concept of "wish-fulfillment," suggesting that these "portals" enable dreams to become a reality. In a text that moves between Kenya, San Francisco, Naples, New York City, and Crandale, *Goon Squad* suggests that the time it takes to traverse space has been reduced in the digital world. However, time, the "goon" of the title, is inescapable for the human body. While the safari-goers can move across large expanses of space to meet again later and connect across vast distances via digital communication, the marker of time is still evident on their bodies: "In a few cases, they'll meet again to reminisce and marvel at one another's physical transformations" (71). *Goon Squad* considers that while the internet may have reduced the time it takes to communicate with one another, neither the physical self nor the material world can escape the effects of time.

Across the roughly fifty years of history that *Goon Squad* covers, the central event is left off the page: the events of September 11, 2001. Sasha is haunted by the space left by the towers, and the final chapter is set in an area called "the Footprint," situated where the towers used to be. As Peter Boxall notes, in many post-9/11 texts the events of that day resonate as "part of the living tissue of the present" (1). This is also a text that depicts a future ravaged by the effects of climate change, with mosquito nets needed in New York, and a world where "warming-related 'adjustments' to Earth's orbit had shortened the winter days, so that now, in January, sunset was taking place at 4:23" (322).[4] The "goon" of time is a unifying force not only through the universal experience of aging, but also through the effects of climate change. As David Wallace-Wells suggests in *The Uninhabitable Earth* (2019), "As conditions of environmental degradation become more universal, it may, perversely, require more imagination to consider their costs" (134). The future of these final two chapters of *Goon Squad* is one born of a lack of imagination; like *Look at Me* before them, they depict what life could look like if America continues on the same path (and as with *Look at Me,* some of what Egan envisions in this text has come to be). The gradual degradation of the characters' health is mirrored by the Earth itself, which by the end of the text is struggling to sustain human life. As Wallace-Wells notes, climate change is sometimes described as "a revenge of time" (202), and it is this broad revenge of time—through the aging of the characters, as well as the destruction of the earth—that is a clear theme throughout *Goon Squad*.

Punk Authenticity

Rather than a break from her earlier work, *Goon Squad* is a continuation and refinement of two interrelated themes that have preoccupied Egan across her career: artistic authenticity and the existential changes brought about by digital technology. Egan's depictions of the punk scene are reminiscent of how she depicts the countercultural movements of the 1960s, in that no character believes they are a true representation of these scenes or are truly experiencing these moments. As Egan is well aware, "authenticity" has some very specific meanings in the context of punk rock. I follow Jesse Prinz's suggestion that, although punk is a heterogeneous label, it nonetheless has three consistent themes: irreverence, nihilism, and amateurism (584–586). All three of these themes are captured by the title of a song by Bennie's teenage band, the Flaming Dildos, called "What the Fuck" (44). In failing to live up to their ideals, many of the characters do not feel that they are truly punks. Egan says of Rhea, the narrator of the chapter "Ask Me If I Care," that she "wants to be real—that's pretty much lifted from my own teenage years" (Kachka). Rhea and her friends think everyone else is more punk than they are. They go to the San Francisco punk club, the Mabuhay Gardens—"the Mab"—in order to be near those they see as authentic punks: "In the Mab's graffiti-splattered bathroom we eavesdrop: Ricky Sleeper fell off the stage at a gig, Joe Rees of Target Video is making an entire movie of punk rock, two sisters we always see at the club have started turning tricks to pay for heroin. Knowing all this makes us one step closer to being real, but not completely" (45–46). They slam dance so that "our sweat is mixed up with real punks' sweat and our skin has actually touched their skin," but touching those they perceive to be real punks will be the limit of their punk authenticity (46). This is largely because Rhea and her friends are unsure at what point someone becomes a punk: "When does a fake Mohawk become a real Mohawk? Who decides? How do you know if it's happened?" (46). A sense of always striving to be real, to be a true punk, permeates much of their teens, and defines many of Bennie's later ideals about music. Rhea is worried about her freckles, and notices that "no punk rockers have freckles" (46). She deems that her friend, Alice (who will later be Scotty's estranged wife) cannot be a punk as "her hair is long and gold" so "she isn't a real punk, either" (47). The punk purity they seek is never quite reached, each character seeing their own punk image as a form of staged authenticity. As discussed in relation to the story "Why China?" in Chapter Two, MacCannell names this process the "dialectic of authenticity." He argues that there is "a collective agreement that reality and truth exist somewhere in society, and that we ought to be trying to find them and refine them" (*The Tourist* 155). The dialectic is this constant desire to experience and refine such moments, but for these young aspiring punks, they can never quite find the truth they seek.

Egan leaps through time in order to interrogate such staged authenticity, here in relation to the apparent demise of punk. She charts the transition from the late-1970s world of punk to the contemporary moment, demonstrating how Bennie's notion of authenticity becomes frozen in time. Jennifer Smith points out, "That Bennie is a has-been punk kid is apt: he works in a genre that loses authenticity the moment it gains an audience" (142). In short, as a music producer, nothing he hears can live up to his ideal, because once it reaches the ears of a music executive like himself whose aim is to refine its authenticity, it has already lost the authenticity he craves. When the reader first meets Bennie in "The Gold Cure," he is particularly annoyed by the digitization of music, and he laments that his nine-year-old son, Chris, "had grown up around rock groups, of course, but he was part of the postpiracy generation, for whom things like 'copyright' and 'creative ownership' didn't exist" (26). But Bennie, as well as not recognizing the irony of a former punk being concerned with copyright law, also fails to reflect on earlier forms of copyright infringement. As a teen, Bennie had no issue with "blasting bootleg tapes of the Stranglers, the Nuns, Negative Trend" as he and his friends drove around San Francisco (39). Bennie's notion of authenticity is frozen in time, and he fails to notice how things he did when he was young are now being repeated, only with slightly different tools. In another instance of repetition, as teens the characters record music in Scotty's garage using Alice's recorder. This is then repeated in "The Gold Cure" when Bennie visits a band he has signed, Stop/Go; Bennie checks that they have the recording software Pro Tools set up so they can record on the spot (29). Technology in both instances refines and completes a process that Bennie's generation started, but he is unable to see these connections because he is concerned with valorizing his own outdated image of musical authenticity.

Bennie's career in music is one that has seen a huge change from analog recording to digital. He claims this has resulted in music being too well made: "The problem was precision, perfection; the problem was *digitization,* which sucked the life out of everything that got smeared through its microscopic mesh. Film, photography, music: dead. *An aesthetic holocaust!* Bennie knew better than to say this stuff aloud" (23). According to Moling, "Digitization, Egan seems to propose, merely produces formulaic simulacra of rock music's erstwhile exciting nuance" (61). Moling and Bennie are misremembering Bennie's teens; while Bennie claims he misses "muddiness, the sense of actual musicians playing actual instruments in an actual room" (22), he was, like his friends, never really a part of this scene, and he was trying to experience something nebulously "real." What he really seems to resent is that the music has changed, but his own musical choices reflect the fact that change is not necessarily a bad thing. As part of the Flaming Dildos, he asks people from "Band and Orchestra" to come join the band, including "a sax, a tuba, and a banjo," as well as Marty, the violinist who joins them onstage when they get to play at the Mab (44). Egan suggests that by pushing their sound in this direction, Bennie is already looking to the "late-eighties sound somewhere between punk and ska" that will become a platinum success with the Conduits (125). Bennie's idea of authenticity is based on a false memory of his teens, and, as a result, he fails to see that many of the issues he complains about—piracy, the lack of melody to the music being produced—are exactly the complaints many had about punk when it first came out.

However, Bennie's management of the band that made him a celebrity, the Conduits, is never shown. His success with this band allows him to sell his label to "multinational crude-oil extractors," and make him enough money to be able to move to Crandale, New York (23).[5] In this sense, Bennie is much more like Thomas Keene from *Look at Me* than he would like to admit, as Keene's choices are defined by the multinational corporations that own his enterprise. Egan explores another instance of authenticity though Bosco, the guitarist for the Conduits, who is seen at length only at the end of his career, in the chapter "A to B." His younger performances were so energetic that "more than once, club owners had called 911 during Conduits shows, convinced that Bosco was having a seizure" (125). By 2006, he has survived cancer, had "an unsuccessful hip operation," and is obese (125). He wants to plan his comeback, and although his publicist—Bennie's wife, Stephanie—is skeptical, his idea is for greater access, for more authenticity: "Let's document every fucking humiliation. This is reality, right? You don't look good anymore twenty years later, especially when you've had half your guts removed. Time's a goon, right? Isn't that the expression?" (127). He plans a "Suicide Tour," where he performs like he used to until his body gives up: "Reality TV, hell—it doesn't get any realer than this. Suicide is a weapon; that we all know. But what about an art?" (129). Bosco wishes to show the world what authentic aging looks like, as well as dying, but once again it is an image of staged authenticity; he wants to prove his authenticity literally onstage, while performing. As Michael Szalay points out, "throughout *Goon Squad,* characters struggle to manufacture moment-defining culture" (269). Here, Bosco wants to show what life looks like after fame and fortune, and to reveal the backstage to the audience. Dorothy Butchard argues, "Thematically, Bosco is a direct successor to Charlotte in *Look at Me,*" as they are similarly wrapped up in "an increasing commercial demand for performed versions of individuals' 'authentic' lives" (368). But as Aaron Derosa aptly notes, "Three years after the September 11 attacks that loom over these stories, Bosco's rationale echoes the logic of the suicide bomber" (98). The artist as terrorist is something DeLillo explores in *Mao II* (1991), and while Bill Gray, the reclusive author of DeLillo's text, concedes that "bomb-makers and gunmen have taken that territory [from novelists]" (41), Bosco hopes that his tour can give punk back its shock factor, through the authentic act of a public suicide. However, that he signs up a writer and Stephanie's brother, Jules Jones, to sculpt and refine his story, means Bosco's supposedly authentic act will be managed and presented by another party.

Indeed, *Goon Squad* is dominated by characters who are managing images of authenticity. The safari trip that Lou takes Mindy and his children on has a guide, Albert, who manages these tourists' experience of Kenya, and as part of this tour the locals put on a show of traditional dancing for the guests. As MacCannell notes of tours, "each one promises real and convincing shows of local life and culture," of which the tourist cannot know what is authentic, and what is a show for them ("Staged" 601). But the staged authenticity of this safari tour extends to other aspects of the plot. There is the genocidal general whose image La Doll—Lulu's mother and Stephanie's boss—is tasked with improving. She does so through asking him to wear a hat and date the actress Kitty Jackson, thereby managing how he is seen by others. As mentioned, Egan has explored characters managing images since her earliest collection, and *Goon Squad* is no different. Indeed, the main text concludes with Scotty's supposedly "pure" performance, which once again has been managed by a particular party to present the image of authenticity. Punk authenticity is shown to be, like the staged authenticity of a safari, managed and sculpted for its intended audience. This constant dialectic of seeking the truth that is somewhere out there, in travel, in music, or in technological connectivity, pervades *Goon Squad* more than any of Egan's previous fiction.

Technology and Privacy

As well as charting the paths of young punks to their later middle-class lives, Egan uses the half a century of time covered in *Goon Squad* to explore the effects of technological advancements, particularly regarding the digital. Zara Dinnen labels this development the "digital banal," which she defines as "the condition by which we don't notice the affective novelty of becoming-with digital media" (*Banal* 1). *Goon Squad* maps this gradual development, situating it as beginning in the early 1970s. In "Safari," the earliest chapter chronologically, Lou's girlfriend, Mindy, is startled by the new "privacy" provided by Lou's "tiny cassette player with a small set of foam earphones" (65). Like Phoebe listening to Barry's cassette player at the end of *The Invisible Circus,* this scene points ahead to numerous technological developments, and Egan catalogues these throughout *Goon Squad*. In 1979, six years later, Bennie and his friends will be driving around San Francisco listening to bootleg tapes, a feat not possible before the 1970s. In the mid-2000s, Bennie comes to lament the collapse of tape, and he loathes the "digitization" of the "postpiracy" generation. In the near future of the final chapter, there has been a baby boom after years of war, and the market has adapted to serve the most populous generation: children use new devices called Starfish to buy music, which, as Butchard has pointed out, is another of Egan's Nostradamus-like predictions, since the mobile app market today is indeed dominated by the demands of children (368). From the cassette player to the Starfish, across the expanse of time represented in *Goon Squad,* Egan explores both this transition to privacy and the monetization of these private choices,. In the near future of "Pure Language," Alex laments that "he never could quite forget that every byte of information he'd posted online (favorite color, vegetable, sexual position) was stored in the databases of multinationals who swore they would never, ever use it" (316). Alex hates the fact that he is "*owned,* in other words, having sold himself unthinkingly at the very point in his life when he'd felt most subversive" (316). That his personal choices are described as "subversive" shows how the idea of personal choice, one that Egan suggests was born from punk, has become embedded into the foundations of this near future of surveillance capitalism.

Artistic purity is a theme that is announced by the title of the final chapter, "Pure Language." Far from a clear statement of pure expression, this chapter explores different iterations of linguistic purity and different understandings of what such a "pure language" entails. Bennie wants to hire Alex to clandestinely promote Scotty's gig because Alex is "a purist," so Bennie considers him "perfect for this" (310). For Bennie, Alex can use this "pure language" to promote his product. In this sense Alex is a mirror of Scotty, who is seen as pure by the crowd that adores him precisely because he "had never had a page or profile or a handle or a handset, who was part of no one's data, a guy who had lived in the cracks all these years, forgotten and full of rage, in a way that now registered as pure. Untouched" (336).[6] Authenticity, then, is shown to be matter of being outside of the market, and Scotty's purity was achieved by years of being poor. As Jeffrey Nealon notes of millennial American capitalism: "authenticity can only be purchased (and make no mistake, authenticity too is a commodity) at the price of utter obscurity" (49). Like the punk that they loved as teenagers, music becomes tainted, impure, as soon as it is performed for money. For Alex, Bennie, and Scotty, authenticity comes from being outside of the market, a position which contradictorily becomes the most marketable commodity. Indeed, Bennie and Alex must conceal their scheme, particularly in the aftermath of the "Bloggescandals," an event that collapsed all trust in political bloggers. Even transparency has not restored trust: "the financial disclosure statements that political bloggers were required to post hadn't stemmed the suspicion that people's opinions weren't really their own. 'Who's paying you?' was a retort that might follow any bout of enthusiasm, along with laughter—who would let themselves be bought?" (315). All enthusiasm is regarded with particular suspicion. In a development of the ideas of trust and sincerity she explored in *The Keep,* Egan returns to *Look at Me*'s themes of how the market influences such online communication, in order to suggest that the trust and sincerity demanded in online communication can always be tainted by a person contacting others for commercial gain.

Conversely, Nicholas Brown argues, "The 'pure language' of the title is the language of the market" (110). Lulu, Bennie's assistant, does not have any "piercings, tattoos, or scarifications" (317); indeed, she is "clean," like "all the kids were now" (317). She is part of a generation, Alex notes, where "no one swore" (320). Lulu's lack of piercings, and the fact that she says words like "gosh," "shucks," and "'golly' . . . without apparent irony," represents a different form of purity dictated by the market: the market of surveillance capitalism (320). For example, as Charlotte found in *Look at Me,* once her life became something that others could track and explore, she began to sober up and monitor her behavior. Similarly, in the digital future Egan depicts in *Goon Squad,* the "purity" of Lulu is one dictated by a market where the self is the commodity; Lulu is a "a living embodiment of the new 'handset employee': Paperless, deskless, commuteless, and theoretically omnipresent" (317). She is, in short, constantly monitored, and her purity is her product. Brown is therefore right to state that the purity of the title is the language of the market, as shown when Lulu dismisses Alex's objection that doing something for money is inherently wrong: "if I believe, I believe. Who are you to judge my reasons?" (320). However, there is also the more insidious suggestion that the world of surveillance capitalism manages and coerces Lulu's generation into being "pure" in this way. The management of purity for a particular audience is much like the desire for authenticity seen throughout Egan's fiction. In the case of Lulu's generation, the policing of all their behavior demands such purity. As Shoshana Zuboff contends, "intervening in the state of play in order to nudge, coax, tune, and herd behavior toward profitable outcomes" is the aim of surveillance capitalism, and those of Lulu's generation have been trained to be the most profitable sources of income they can be (*Surveillance* 8). In this sense, their bodies and speech represent the pure language of the market.

In the final scenes, Scotty performs his concert to an adoring public, to a crowd orchestrated by Bennie. This has been achieved through the use of Alex and his "parrots" (315)—friends he has asked Lulu to contact to promote this performance—to create this moment. Michael Szalay argues that this final scene is really a "triumph of marketing" (269), while Katherine Johnston points out that Scotty's show is promoted to create a complicated notion of authenticity: "Scotty's purity is heavily produced, promoted, and protected, so that living off the grid becomes a fashion statement or publicity stunt that is itself advertised through the grid and authenticated within profile society" (170). Johnston discusses the rise of "profile culture," meaning the world in which everyone curates their profiles online. To build from Johnston's insights, profile culture—like the world of PersonalSpace seen in *Look at Me*—is supposed to provide unfiltered access to everyone's lives; however, Egan shows how online profiles are another world of staged authenticity. The dialectic of authenticity then switches, leading to a collective understanding of authenticity as something achieved by those outside of profile culture, and Scotty's performance is needed as "two generations of war and surveillance had left people craving the embodiment of their own unease in the form of a lone, unsteady man on a slide guitar" (335). As with the car crash near the end of *Look at Me* or Holly's visit to Howard's hotel in *The Keep, Goon Squad* finishes with an image of staged authenticity. But, like Holly's experiences, this performance is redemptive for "young people like Lulu, who was now holding hands with a statuesque black man, both of them gazing at Scotty Hausmann with the rhapsodic joy of a generation finally descrying someone worthy of its veneration" (336). The authenticity may be staged and managed, but the value of this performance is one that passes into "myth," to the extent that "more people claim [they were at the concert] . . . than could possibly have fit into the space, capacious and mobbed though it was" (336). Like La Doll's disastrous party in which Kitty reveals people have burned themselves to pretend they were there, the claim of having been present at this era-defining moment becomes more important than the substance of Scotty's art. His performance, however managed and manufactured for the crowd, is a historical moment: "And it may be that a crowd at a particular moment of history creates the object to justify its gathering, as it did at the first Human Be-In and Monterey Pop and Woodstock" (335). As Scotty is beloved by this new "pure" generation, the end of "Pure Language" suggests that a new era—one defined by climate change, surveillance, and war—requires new figures of veneration.

After Scotty's performance, the tangle of the plot forms one last connection, and one that loops round back to the start. Alex speaks to Bennie about Sasha, who has long since stopped being his assistant. They decide to visit her old apartment, on the Lower East Side, but no one answers. Alex wonders what has happened to him in the intervening years, and Bennie answers, "You grew up, Alex . . . just like the rest of us" (340). Time, aging, and maturity are therefore emphasized in the final pages, and giving up on a pure language is shown to be part of growing up in *Goon Squad*. The main text finishes with Alex and Bennie hearing "clicking heels on the pavement," and they both turn, "peering for Sasha in the ashy dark" (340). But it is not Sasha: "it was another girl, young and new to the city, fiddling with her keys" (340). In this final scene, Egan depicts another young person moving to the city to try and make something of themselves, much like Sasha and Alex, and so the tangle of *Goon Squad* ends with the narrative returning to where it started.

Black Box

Egan decided to return to the world of *Goon Squad* for "Black Box," a much-discussed short story she released on the *New Yorker* Twitter account in 2012. A far cry from the tone of *Goon Squad,* the story is what Egan defines as a "spy-thriller," fulfilling a "long-term goal" of taking "a character from a naturalistic story and travel[ing] with her into a different genre" ("Coming Soon"). Here, Egan takes Lulu and transplants her into the 2030s, on a secret mission to infiltrate and gather information from a group of criminals. Lulu is a temporary cyborg; her body has been modified for this mission. She has a recording device planted inside herself, so Lulu's body is the "black box" of the title. Like *The Keep,* "Black Box" is a found text, with Egan leaving its context ambiguous; the reader never knows whether Lulu survives at the end, or whether this information has been retrieved from her corpse. Egan tells the story in the second person and in the form of a list, a structure she had long been interested in and had briefly experimented with in 2003 with a "20-Minute Story" for Dave Eggers's *McSweeney's* ("Jennifer Egan To Do"). Although "Black Box" was published separately, it should be understood as part of *Goon Squad*; to push the album structure metaphor a little further, "Black Box" can be understood as a hidden track, like the songs placed on vinyl records and CDs after a period of silence following the last track. Labeling it a hidden track fits thematically with the silences that Sasha's son is obsessed with in the chapter "Great Rock and Roll Pauses," and the idea of a hidden track also fits conceptually with the clandestine nature of Lulu's mission.[7]

"Black Box" is structured as forty-seven short chapters, and it was written in what Egan names the "odd poetry that can happen in a hundred and forty characters" ("Coming Soon"). The serialized format is part of a broader turn by contemporary writers to the serial form, as evident in Michael Chabon's *Gentlemen of the Road* (2007), which was released weekly in the *New Yorker* in 2007 (like Egan, he also planned it all ahead of time rather than writing it as each issue was published). There have been other experiments with Twitter and fiction; as Jennifer Gutman points out, Neil Gaiman, Elliot Holt, and Teju Cole all produced Twitter fiction in 2009, 2012, and 2014 respectively (27). "Black Box" finds Egan once again experimenting with genre and form, and it is another story in the *Goon Squad* saga that follows its own set of rules distinct from any other chapter. The plot itself is quite simple: It follows Lulu as she infiltrates a group of unnamed men, specifically monitoring her "Designated Mate" and trying to remain undetected as she records his conversations and downloads information from his computer. The premise is remarkably similar to the short-lived Fox show *Dollhouse* (2009–2010), in which young women are used for spying, sexual gratification (Lulu has been taught a "dissociation technique" to remain absent during the sex these men demand), and whatever desires people have. At the end of "Black Box" Lulu's cover is blown, she is shot in the shoulder, and the final scene is of her on a boat, waiting to be rescued by a helicopter.

Despite being keenly interested in the existential effects wrought by technological developments, at the time of "Black Box" Egan was not someone who Tweeted. As with the PowerPoint chapter, "Great Rock and Roll Pauses"—which she originally sketched by hand—Egan had no real experience with Twitter before publishing her work of "Twitterature." In a conversation with the artist Sarah Sze, Egan explains how she began this project: "I started out by joining Twitter and I discovered that I really wasn't comfortable tweeting. I didn't feel like I had a voice or a way to do it" (Sze 115). In fact, she admits that she "tweeted four times, and then someone hacked into my Twitter handle and spewed out a bunch of vitamin advertisements; I realized that I had basically only tweeted spam" (115). So, Egan, now seen by many as a pioneer of Twitter fiction, had limited experience with the platform, although she does now have a Twitter presence. In fact, she approached it like any of her other fiction; the story was in no way mapped out, and she worked "from a very large idea to a very specific idiosyncratic detail" (115). Many of these details relate to Lulu's physical transformations, such as a recording device she activates by "pressing the triangle of cartilage" in her "ear canal," or a "Universal Port" between her toes ("Black Box"). The changes to Lulu's body and the technological future connect this story to ideas of the posthuman, in particular to the definitions outlined by Katherine Hayles in *How We Became Posthuman: Virtual Bodies in Cybernetics, Literature, and Informatics* (1999). According to Hayles, "In the posthuman, there are no essential differences or absolute demarcations between bodily existence and computer simulation, cybernetic mechanism and biological organism, robot teleology and human goals" (3). What Egan shows in "Black Box" is that the collapse in the barrier between the human and the cybernetic has dramatic effects for the autonomy of the person who has been modified. The human body is made a vessel for the needs of the state; there is a long list of what defines "the new heroism," where "the goal is to merge with something larger than yourself . . . to throw off generations of self-involvement . . . to renounce the American fixation with being seen and recognized . . . to dig beneath your shiny persona" ("Black Box"). Lulu's sense of self is almost entirely erased; while in *Goon Squad* Alex's defining characteristics are controlled by companies, in "Black Box" the body becomes a site which is monitored, adapted, and controlled by the needs of the American security state.

As Gutman notes, such features are reminiscent of Donna Haraway's descriptions of the cyborg, a figure of both liberation and control: "On the one hand, the protagonist encapsulates a dystopic future world at war where women's bodies are employed as weapons of defense" (275). In this sense, Egan extends the images of coercion and control from *Look at Me,* where a virtual representation of Charlotte's body is sold to the production company and she can no longer be herself. But the cyborg is a more complicated figure than the simulation, and in "Black Box" this is especially so as Lulu's enhancements are temporary: "Technology has afforded ordinary people a chance to glow in the cosmos of human achievement," for a brief time at least ("Black Box"). This militaristic future is dystopian, but Gutman usefully explains why Haraway's cyborg figure is a contradictory image: "On the other hand, her temporary cyborg existence . . . represents a productive synergy with technology that also makes apparent deeper recesses of primal human power that technological add-ons can neither fully eradicate nor rival" (275). That the story is told entirely in the second person captures the uneasy space in which Lulu finds herself; she is physically enhanced, but, as Daniel Aureliano Newman points out, "her empowerment is equivocal at best, her apparent agency belied by her husband and government standing behind the scenes, pulling the strings" (56). The second-person narration is also another instance of the internalization of surveillance seen in *Look at Me,* where behavior is modified once a person feels like they are being surveilled. We only receive glimpses of Lulu's personality, like when she thinks, "You will reflect on the fact that these 'instructions' are becoming less and less instructive" ("Black Box"). As the "clean" product of the surveillance state we meet in "Pure Language," Lulu is used to seeing herself in the second person, as not having a voice that belongs to herself.

Gutman and Newman both see the story as an extension of surveillance capitalism (although they do not name it as such), where, in Gutman's words, "Egan ironically weaponizes the misogynist practice of reducing women to sex objects while linking this entrenched form of patriarchal abuse to a newer mode of subjection that exploits web users as generators of salable content" (281). This is indeed the case, as Lulu's subjectivity during this mission is public, represented through the second-person narration of the story. Lulu's body is more important to the state than her consciousness: "Remember that, should you die, you will have triumphed merely by delivering your physical person into our hands" ("Black Box"). Lulu's subjective self is not the priority; it is rather her physical being, as a posthuman object, that is prized. By adding this story to the world of *Goon Squad,* Egan extends its history of personal recording devices that first began with the cassette that amazes Mindy with the "privacy" afforded by headphones, culminating in the body becoming a recording device in “Black Box,” where all privacy has been removed in favor of “something larger than yourself.”

As well as being a radical formal experiment unlike any of her previous work, *Goon Squad* also summarizes many of the concerns seen in all of her previous fiction: the importance of the 1970s in defining the present, the way staged authenticity leads to ever greater “pseudo-events,” and the role of digital technology in modifying how we understand ourselves and interact with each other. It is particularly concerned with the effects of these changes on the body. To use a musical term, it is a contrapuntal text, meaning it has more than two melodic lines, and no clear protagonists. Indeed, Egan’s next novel, the sweeping historical drama *Manhattan Beach* (2017), is in many ways a much more radical departure by virtue of being her most conventional work, as well as her first text set before the 1970s.

7

Manhattan Beach

For Egan's next work of fiction, she sought to "renounce the tools" of her previous work and write in a new genre, setting, and form (Cooke). In 2012 she again switched publishers, this time from Doubleday to Scribner, signing a reported seven figure publishing deal for the rights to her next two books (Kaufman). She also published book reviews for the *New York Times,* and in many ways cemented her place as a public intellectual. Published on October 3, 2017, to nearly universally positive reviews, *Manhattan Beach* won the American Library Association's Andrew Carnegie Medal for the best work of fiction in 2018, and it was Longlisted for the National Book Award. In the academy, in 2019 an entire issue of the journal *PMLA* was dedicated to *Manhattan Beach,* concluding with a short response by Egan to the readings collected in the issue. In short, the reaction to *Manhattan Beach* from publishers, the literary press, awards committees, and academia, demonstrates the central place Egan now occupies in American letters.

I begin this chapter with a plot summary, before explaining the exhaustive research that went into this novel. I then connect many of the interpretations and complaints about the historical authenticity of *Manhattan Beach* through Richard Dyer's theories of pastiche. For Dyer pastiche is "inescapably historical" (Dyer 131). Dyer defines pastiche as the "aesthetic imitation" of a historical period, and by drawing on the genres of noir and the seafaring novel, Egan creates a pastiche of 1940s Brooklyn (1). The staged authenticity present in this novel, then, is part of the pastiche of this historical moment that Egan produces. The historical setting of *Manhattan Beach* echoes Dyer's description of pastiche as occupying an "uncertain, but suggestive and productive place," as it is set at a moment in America's history when it was on the cusp of dramatic change (54). *Manhattan Beach* explores the moment when the American

Century was about to begin; set in the years 1934 to 1945, it is both a post-Depression story and a war novel, one that explores America at a moment of radical societal shifts in regard to gender, race, and class. As Egan told Allan Vorda: "The war in general was such a time of tumult. Women's lives were one of many different kinds of accepted patterns that were disrupted. I think that a lot of what happened in the '60s, in terms of the civil rights movements and all kinds of other things, were the result of that disruption." Building from Walter Scheidel's concepts in his work *The Great Leveler: Violence and the History of Inequality from the Stone Age to the Twenty-First Century* (2018), I contend that *Manhattan Beach* is a text that explores a moment of shock, of a transition to a different social order. However, like the mode of pastiche in which it is written, the historical moment it captures is uncertain. Just as in *The Invisible Circus* or *Goon Squad,* the novel's huge event—in *Manhattan Beach* this is the war—happens off the page. *Manhattan Beach* is reflective of the huge changes not only at home in relation to new social dynamics, but also around the world in terms of the global superpower the United States would become after the war. I conclude by arguing that while the Second World War may have led to the beginning of the American Century, Egan suggests that the end of this period may soon be coming.

Manhattan Beach has three plot strands which intersect with different genres. The protagonist is Anna Kerrigan, a young Irish American woman who works at the Brooklyn Navy Yard during the war. She is one of Egan's most typical heroines, in that her narrative arc is one of triumph; namely, she achieves her goal of becoming a diver in Brooklyn Harbor before moving away and forming a life of her own. Then there is the gangster Dexter Styles, whose narrative represents the noir elements of the plot. Finally, there is Anna's father, Eddie Kerrigan, who works for Dexter and ties Anna and Dexter's lives together; he melds Anna's naturalistic moments with Dexter's noir, and he also has his own seafaring adventure. The earliest scenes are set in 1934, with the then-eleven-year-old Anna visiting the house of Dexter Styles with her father. Styles is part of "the Syndicate," a real-life organized crime group that, as T. J. English explains in *Paddy Whacked: The Untold Story of the Irish American Gangster* (2005), was a "consortium of multiethnic mobsters" who fought over the rights to docks and shipping in the first half of the twentieth century (7). In the noir and seafaring side of the story, Anna's father, Eddie, initially works in the Irish American world of organized crime as a bagman. Egan builds this world out of her research into what historian James Fisher describes—in a book Egan cites as a huge influence on the text—as the convoluted and corrupt world of "gangster[s], priest[s], and cop[s] alike" of the New York waterfronts in the 1940s (34). Eddie moves into the Syndicate's mafia world as

Dexter's "eyes and ears," which involves acquiring information on people that Dexter wishes to learn more about (315). Connecting this idea of surveillance to her earlier fiction, Egan suggests that the tactics of surveillance capitalism, which she explored in *Look at Me, The Keep,* and *Goon Squad,* were previously employed by the mob. Dexter works for a man called simply Mr. Q., whose front is a vegetable farm upstate, but behind this façade "the tendons of his power stretched from Bensonhurst to Albany to Niagara Falls, Kansas City, New Orleans, [and] Miami" (189). Dexter made his name during the years of Prohibition, and now largely runs nightclubs—initially as a means to dispense the liquor they have left over since the end of Prohibition in 1933—as well as some other "less legal" practices (157). Dexter is a Gatsby-like figure who has changed his name from its "unpronounceable" Italian heritage to something that is not subtle in redefining him as a man of style (203). Dexter's father-in-law, Arthur Berringer, is a prominent banker, and Dexter longs for the legitimacy of his father-in-law's life. Eddie is never comfortable with his surveillance work, and after the murder of his former employer, the shady union boss John Dunellen, he becomes an informant to state prosecutors. Dexter finds this out and decides he has to kill Eddie to guarantee his silence. But Eddie, a former vaudeville star, performs an elaborate Houdini-like escape, unshackling himself from his chains after being thrown into the ocean. He is dragged out of the water by a kindly Norwegian fisherman and escapes into the merchant marines, an arm of the war operation that, as historian Brian Herbert points out, had "more deaths per capita in that war than any of the American armed forces" (13). Indeed, Eddie's sister, Brianne, calls the merchant marines "the real heroes" toward the end, and *Manhattan Beach* is partially a recognition of the sacrifices of this underacknowledged branch of the armed forces during the Second World War (415). As a merchant marine, Eddie loses his ship, the *Elizabeth Seaman,* in an ambush by German U-Boats.[1] Stranded, he is left for weeks on a raft with only a bosun from Nigeria for company, a man with whom he was previously at loggerheads. In these scenes, the text becomes a "lost at sea" story. Eddie is incredibly close to death by the time he is rescued, and at the end of the text he is reunited with Anna in San Francisco.

Anna's side of the plot begins in 1934. She is at Dexter's house; her father is hoping to begin working for Dexter in order to pay for a wheelchair for Lydia, Anna's disabled sister. Starved of oxygen at birth, Lydia has severe cerebral palsy, and cannot communicate or move. Three years later, Eddie disappears, believed to have run away. The reader next meets Anna as a 19-year-old in 1942, living with her mother, Agnes, a former dancer for the Ziegfeld Follies, and Lydia. Anna works at the shipyard doing rote tasks, and here she makes a friend, Nell, who takes her out one night to a nightclub owned by Dexter. In another example of the remarkable coincidences that litter Egan's work, on this night out Anna bumps into Dexter. Anna then witnesses people diving in the harbor to repair warships, and longs to try it herself, the control of oxygen that this activity entails having a clear connection to the lack of oxygen Lydia had at birth. Anna is initially rebuffed because of her gender but is given the chance to try diving through the kindly interventions of her closeted boss, Charles Voss, and passes the test. Against the wishes of a misogynistic lieutenant, Anna becomes part of the diving team at the Brooklyn Naval Yard. After she meets Dexter again, they organize a day at the beach for Lydia. Here, in one of the most startling scenes in the novel, seeing the water triggers Lydia to speak for the first time. In a manner that recalls how in *Goon Squad* Rhea and Jocelyn take the ailing Lou outside for one last look at his pool, water here is central to a moment of transition between life and death. Indeed, Lydia dies soon after this outing, leaving a void for Anna's mother, who then moves back to Minnesota to live with her family. On another night out with Nell, Dexter invites Anna to come meet him, and she does. After sex in the same boathouse where he plans many of his executions, Anna reveals to Dexter she has lied that her last name is Feeney; moreover, that she had met him before, and she asks Dexter if he knows what happened to her father. Dexter takes Anna diving at the spot where he had Eddie's body thrown overboard, and Anna finds Eddie's watch on the ocean floor, which she believes confirms the time of his death. Dexter is then murdered by Badger, a fellow gangster he has disrespected numerous times. Why he is killed is left uncertain—possibly because his affair with Anna breaks his promise to his father-in-law to never cheat on his daughter, or possibly because Mr. Q. believes he is a threat to their way of life, as Dexter is considering coming out of the hidden world of organized crime to buy war bonds. After his death, Anna discovers that she is pregnant with Dexter's baby. Through Nell, she plans an abortion, but in a melodramatic change of mind, she stops the procedure at the last moment. Her aunt, Brianne, helps her to make up a believable story, and Anna uses her savings to move to San Francisco. Here, she meets up with Eddie again, begins diving in the San Francisco harbor, and has a son, Leon. The entire novel takes place over the years 1934 to 1945, and except for the scenes on Eddie's boat and the final section in California, it is set entirely in New York.

New York and Connections to Egan's Earlier Fiction

Manhattan Beach was the result of what George Hutchinson has called a "maniacal" level of research, as the voluminous acknowledgements found at the end of the text attest (391). Such research is deeply indebted to an oral history project Egan undertook with the Brooklyn Navy Yard and Brooklyn Historical

Society. But the influence of her nonfiction was also part of the process; as she said to Rachel Cooke, journalism "has taught me how to distil enormous quantities of information, and I wouldn't have been able to write *Manhattan Beach* without that because I have never scuba dived. Actually, I've barely been on a ship." Her research was not only archival—she tried on a 200-pound diving suit from the era, and also interviewed many divers regarding their experiences ("International Writers"). However, the novel is not a complete break from *Goon Squad*; while that work looked at the aftermath of 9/11, *Manhattan Beach* is partly inspired by a desire to look at what she felt in New York during 9/11: "the feeling of New York having been invaded" and turned into a "warzone" was something Egan wanted to delve into (Paul). She discusses the ways 9/11 "made me think about the trajectory of American global power, and wonder about the future of that trajectory, but also . . . wonder about the past of it: which really was, World War Two" (Paul). Of particular interest to her was the fact that America ended World War Two "unscathed . . . and incredibly strong" (Paul). After exploring the period from the 1960s to the present (and beyond) in her previous fiction, *Manhattan Beach* is the first work of Egan's fiction to be set in a time before her own birth in 1962.

Manhattan Beach situates Egan as a New York writer. While *Goon Squad* laments the overdevelopment of New York, with the final images of a skyscraper obscuring Alex and Rebecca's view from their apartment—Alex watches with dread as the development begins to "seal off their air and light" (314)—*Manhattan Beach* is a book that looks at the beginnings of this transition, of New York's burgeoning dominance in the financial and cultural world.[2] But the novel is also more localized than *Goon Squad*, and delineates Egan as one of many contemporary writers who call Brooklyn their home. Like Jonathan Lethem's *Motherless Brooklyn* (1999) or Paul Auster's *The Brooklyn Follies* (2005), *Manhattan Beach* focuses on this particular borough of New York. Evan Hughes explored this recent trend in depth in *Literary Brooklyn: The Writers of Brooklyn and the Story of American City Life* (2011), and the tendency for writers to move to Brooklyn became a topic of Michael Maren's film *A Short History of Decay* (2013), in which Egan can briefly be seen in the background. Egan's novel is particularly focused on the waterfronts of this city, which have long been a topic of literary intrigue, most notably in Walt Whitman's poem "Crossing Brooklyn Ferry" (1856). However, if Whitman's vision is preoccupied with the surface of the New York waterfront and the people on it, Egan's text is dominated by the city's depths and shadow worlds; Anna becomes a diver fixing ships, and Dexter Styles refers to organized crime as "the shadow world" (and the entire second section is titled "Shadow World"). In Egan's text, New York—as it is in *Look at Me*—is a space of shiny surfaces concealing hidden depths. *Manhattan Beach* is also a further acknowledgment of the centrality of New York to her life; after coming to New York in her twenties and struggling to establish herself, *Manhattan Beach* is Egan confirming that "I stayed and became a New Yorker, really" (Chamberlin).

The waterfronts of New York also point to Egan's wider preoccupation with water throughout her fiction. Water is both a setting of death—Faith's suicide in *The Invisible Circus* or Rob's drowning in *Goon Squad*—and redemption, as in Holly's dive into the imagination pool in *The Keep*. In *Manhattan Beach,* it is both life-giving, such as when seeing the water enlivens Lydia to speak for the first time, and also a place of death, quite literally, in that Dexter dumps his bodies in the sea. As Fisher notes: "The annual April crop of bloated corpses surfacing after a winter submerged in the frosty Hudson was a harbinger of spring" (xii). In this image, the New York waterfronts signal the start of spring, and also act as a reminder of the city's dark world of organized crime. In *Manhattan Beach,* the waterways of New York represent the allegorical world of surface and depth that filters through the entire text. For instance, "Each time Anna moved from her father's world to her mother and Lydia's, she felt as if she'd shaken free of one life for a deeper one" (26). Anna finds there is no end to how far she can go: "Back and forth she went, deeper—deeper still—until it seemed there was no place further down she could go. But somehow there always was. She had never reached the bottom" (26). Such language foreshadows Anna's diving, which serves as a clear metaphor for this two-tier world. Indeed, as mentioned, one of the possible reasons Dexter dies is that he tries to emerge from the shadow world and seek "legitimacy," thereby breaking the balance of this allegorical world that Egan has created (197).

Eddie's descent into the shadow world is the result of pulling someone out of water; before working for Dexter, he was given work by Dunellen after saving him "along with another protectory boy" from drowning (27). Allan Hepburn points out, "Throughout *Manhattan Beach,* being in or near the ocean initiates transformations, although they are often ambiguous" (388). Water serves as a variable metaphor throughout the text, for as John Fabian Witt puts it: "The tides bring experience, not language. They deliver peace and death. They can be ecstatic and life-creating, or dangerous and deadly" (414). Eddie's experiences encapsulate this multifarious nature. For instance, he realizes that "much of his own speech derived from the sea," with common phrases like "keeled over," "learning the ropes," "catching the drift," "freeloader," and "gripe" all being nautical idioms (260). But the ocean is not only a place that begets language; it also represents what is beyond language, as Dexter finds when he dives with Anna: "This was the primeval dark of nightmares. It covered secrets too atrocious to be exposed: drowned children, sunken ships" (339). Indeed, to return to Witt, he points out that in *Manhattan Beach* "the ocean figures as a space beyond language—sometimes, at least" (414). Nevertheless, water has featured in Egan's fiction from her earliest short stories as a site of intrigue and as a multipurpose metaphor. *Manhattan Beach,* while it does break new ground for Egan, also makes clearer than ever her preoccupations with depths and surfaces through the allegorical world of the New York waterfronts.

While the majority of the novel is set in New York, the final scenes, which are set in San Francisco, affirm Egan's status as a bicoastal writer. Indeed, one early plan for her next project, since aborted, was to follow Anna Kerrigan's son to write "the sort of sixties novel no one wrote, the one I wish I could have read, that captures what it was like to live then" (Schwartz). Here, Egan points to the ways *Manhattan Beach* hearkens back to her debut novel, *The Invisible Circus*; both are historical novels that follow young women as they try to find an absent family member—in Phoebe's case, her sister, but in Anna's case, her father. Both are also works of historical fiction that attempt to capture a particular era of American history. Like Phoebe, Anna compares herself to Alice going through the looking glass: "She felt like Alice in Wonderland, fitting herself through smaller and smaller doors with no idea where they might lead" (157). The passionate sex that Anna has with Dexter also echoes Phoebe and Wolf's tumultuous affair, and the fact that Wolf was the last to see Faith alive is mirrored in Dexter believing he was the last to see Eddie. The ideas of image and performance found in *Look at Me* are also evident in the text, as Tabitha, Dexter's daughter, is seen in one scene to be glaring into her vanity mirror. Tabitha is also obsessed with the stars and celebrities who appear in her father's clubs, and she always asks who has frequented them recently. Similarly, Anna's mother, Agnes, first moved to New York to work as a dancer in the Follies, further suggesting that some of the elements of the image culture Egan explores in her earlier fiction are present in this text in embryonic form. Egan has also described the importance of *The Keep* to her ability to write a work outside of her experience, as that Gothic text was, like *Manhattan Beach,* "a world she had to invent" (Paul). As Janet Lyon perceptively points out, Eddie's inability to communicate with his disabled daughter, Lydia, is similar to Drew's difficulties communicating with his autistic son, Lincoln, in *Goon Squad* (409). Finally, Anna's use of a diving suit and her reliance on others for her safety mirror the posthumanism found in "Black Box," where new technology troubles the boundaries between human and non-human.

Perhaps the clearest thematic consistency from her previous fiction is that *Manhattan Beach* is full of twins, doubles, and shadows. The doubling begins in the first chapter; not only are Dexter's sons twins, but Egan also introduces a more abstract sense of doubling here. Dexter considers his potential employee,

Eddie Kerrigan, to have "a shadow, a sorrow. Then again, who hadn't one? Or several?" (9). Each character leads a double life, most obviously Dexter Styles and his "shadow world." Dexter is particularly perturbed by Mackey, who comes to his house, breaking the barrier between the two worlds: "Maintaining an appearance mattered as much—more—than what was underneath. The deeper things could come and go, but what broke the surface would be lodged in everyone's memory" (96). The novel also, like *Goon Squad,* ends with an image of recursion, as Eddie is "disoriented" to see the same "athletic walk" in Anna that he associates with Agnes, Anna's mother (429). Similarly, Anna's disabled sister, Lydia, is twinned and doubled in many ways; from the opening scenes of the novel, Anna longs for the doll with "the blue irises [that] slid" that Tabitha, Dexter's daughter, owns (10). Lydia is seen by Eddie as doll-like, as having no depths: "Her bright blue eyes sought his: clear, perfect eyes that bore no trace of her affliction" (15). Later in the text, Eddie thinks, "the shadow of what [Lydia] should have been clung to her always, a reproachful twin" (267). Aside from being a questionable image of disability—which I will return to later—Eddie sees Lydia as all surface, failing to understand that she does have a personality. It is fitting that what brings her to life is the sea, the defining image of depth and surface throughout the text. When Lydia sees the ocean near Dexter's house, "the Landrace fell from her face as she confronted the sea, lips moving, like a mythical creature whose imprecations could summon storms and winged gods, her wild blue eyes fixed on eternity" (164). Water serves as a clear metaphor for the subterranean worlds that dominated New York during this time period. Finally, Anna's palindromic name looking the same read both backwards and forwards embodies the twins and doubles that proliferate throughout the text.

Historical Authenticity: Bovarysme and Pastiche

After the mosaic-like structure of *Goon Squad,* Egan said she found it particularly challenging to maintain the "momentum" that a piece of historical fiction requires (Cooke). She confesses that when writing *Manhattan Beach,* she discovered that "for me, verisimilitude is actually harder than formal trickiness" (Egan and Saunders). Beginning research in 2004 but not writing a word until 2012 (when her new publishing deal was signed), Egan has cited the writers she was "in conversation with" when writing this novel as "Hilary Mantel, Herman Melville, and Joseph Conrad, and the classic noir writers from the 30s and 40s" ("International Writers"). Dexter is in many ways similar to Thomas Cromwell in Mantel's Henry VIII trilogy, a self-made man who rises to a position of notable power. Another connection to Mantel's historical fiction can be seen in the chronology of the text. In contrast to the convoluted detective work needed to trace the timeline of *Goon Squad,* in *Manhattan Beach* Egan provides extensive dates and historical markers throughout. As Christian Lorentzen waggishly notes in his review of the latter, "*Manhattan Beach* is a novel that grabs the reader by the lapels forcefully and says, 'It's 1942, and don't you forget it!'" The epigraph to the text—"Yes, as everyone knows, meditation and water are wedded forever"—is drawn from Ishmael's opening discussion in *Moby-Dick* (1851) of the vitality and rich experiences that water can bring, which, as noted, is a central theme of *Manhattan Beach* (Melville 4). As well this thematic connection, *Moby-Dick* most obviously influences the seafaring scenes, as well as the encyclopedic, exacting detail about diving, which echoes the long passages of cetology found in Melville's work. But the connection is broader than this, for as Hepburn points out: "In its blending of history with individuals' stories, *Manhattan Beach* can be called an epic novel, along the lines of Herman Melville's *Moby-Dick* and Don DeLillo's *Libra*" (384). As well as once again acknowledging Egan's huge debt to DeLillo, Hepburn usefully connects *Manhattan Beach* to a tradition where "historical change is treated as an epic trope" (384), and in which characters experience huge personal changes at a moment of historical transition. Finally, in relation to Conrad, as well as his seafaring adventure novellas—"Typhoon" (1902) and "Falk" (1903) most clearly—*Manhattan Beach* clearly echoes *Lord Jim* (1900), not only in the way the crew abandons their ship the way Eddie has to, but also in how Jim's delusions of heroism are mirrored in Anna's consumption of mysteries and gangster films. She has an archetypal experience of "Bovarysme," the idea that characters, like the eponymous hero of Gustave Flaubert's *Madame Bovary* (1856), are surprised when the world around them does not quite fit the forms and styles of the novels they read or the films they watch. It is this blend of historical exactitude, epic scope, and the disjunction of art and reality that Egan draws on to create *Manhattan Beach*.

As well as *The Merchant Marine's Officers' Handbook* (1942), which got her "some quizzical looks on the elliptical machine," Egan spent months reading archives of letters written during the war ("By the Book"). She describes how the letters of Lucille "Lucy" Kolkin were one particularly affecting discovery, and Lucy's life appears to serve as a partial model for Anna's, as Lucy moved from Brooklyn, where she was a shipfitter during the war, to California at the end of the war. In Egan's discussion of Lucy, she shows her grasp of the historical facts of the Brooklyn Naval Yard, pointing out that it "built 17 battleships and repaired 5,000, including allied ships from all over the world. And by January 1945, there were 4,657 women at the yard, working in nearly every phase of shipbuilding and repair" (24). Jordynn Jack puts this number in a broader perspective, noting that "between 1941 and 1944, over 6.5 million women joined the workforce" (398). Jack also points out that "Egan has written a book that generally hews to the historical record, except in terms of Anna's unlikely success as a diver" (404). Indeed, the first documented female diver was not until 1981, Mary Motley Crabtree, whom Egan interviewed when developing this work (436). Anna's story, then—diving aside—is based in the huge historical changes wrought by the wartime economy and the radically shifting role of women in society. That Anna works alongside a black man, Marle, and Eddie becomes acquainted with the bosun, a Nigerian, also points to the shifting racial world *Manhattan Beach* depicts.

Depicting America during this maelstrom of change led some reviewers to wonder what Egan was trying to say about the era. For instance, Anne Diebel situated the text in opposition to her earlier fiction: "while *The Invisible Circus* addresses the making of eras, *Manhattan Beach* is vaguer about its own undertaking." But it is precisely the sense of being on the cusp of change that Egan explores in *Manhattan Beach*. In depicting the decade from 1934 to 1945, Egan avoids what Nicholas Dames calls—discussing the periodization of the 1970s in recent fiction—clear "decade-ism," which he defines as "the artistic practice of parceling out history in ten-year spans ("Seventies"). *Manhattan Beach,* in being set from 1934 to 1945, avoids such easy classifications; it is, like so much of Egan's fiction, betwixt and between moments and ideas, and it unsettles historical assumptions. Dames notes, "There is a menu of decades to choose from, and an audience with sophisticated tastes in recent period detail waiting to sample the latest clever, self-aware tweaking of classic ingredients" ("Seventies"). *Manhattan Beach* focuses on the events leading up to momentous changes in women's rights, civil rights, and America's place in the world, rather than representing these changes directly; if *The Invisible Circus* looked at the aftermath of the sixties, *Manhattan Beach* is concerned with the genesis of that era. Egan's historical fiction, then, is purposely defamiliarizing of the era it explores, and it challenges readers' assumptions of how to understand the progress of history.

Dames's focus on "Seventies Throwback Fiction" also points to the broader turn to historical fiction among Egan and her contemporaries. As well as Mantel's blockbuster successes, there have been numerous other contemporary works of historical fiction, such as Thomas Pynchon's *Mason & Dixon* (1997), Ian McEwan's *Atonement* (2001), Susan Choi's *American Woman* (2003), Philip Roth's *The Plot Against America* (2004), Colson Whitehead's *The Underground Railroad* (2016), George Saunders's *Lincoln in the Bardo* (2017), Sarah Waters's numerous neo-Victorian novels, and Michael Chabon's two novels set during World War Two—*The Amazing Adventures of Kavalier and Clay* (2000) and *Moonglow* (2016). Egan's text fits into what Elodie Rousselot has labeled a "new wave of 'neo-historical fiction'" (2). Egan's text does appear to be a part of this "wave," and even has some direct references to her contemporaries. For instance, in Eddie's dramatic escape from being thrown to his death by Dexter, he uses "a few tricks from his vaudeville days: razors in the lining of his trousers, a lock pick nestled between his jaw and gum," a nod to the escapist skills of Josef Kavalier from Chabon's *Kavalier and Clay* (358). Similarly, when Brianne, Anna's aunt, complains that she wished Charles Lindbergh had run for president, Egan is here referencing Roth's alternate history in *The Plot Against America* (112). Egan not only fits *Manhattan Beach* within a broader move across contemporary fiction toward the historicist mode, but also slyly acknowledges the connections between this text and those of her contemporaries. Mitchum Huehls distinguishes numerous subgenres within these recent works of historical fiction: "the residually postmodern historical novel counterbalanced by its realist counterpart, the historical novel of the present, the speculatively generic historical novel, and the historical novel of futurity" (148). But, disparate as these subgenres are in their approaches to history, Huehls argues that there is one thing uniting them: "it's a shared attempt to think the present historically in a moment marked by the end of any strong sense of the past" (148). Contrary to Huehls, I argue—as I did in my discussion of *The Invisible Circus*—that this wave of historical fiction in fact demonstrates that recent fiction cannot stop thinking historically. Rather, the question to ask about texts like *Manhattan Beach* is how they represent and consider the past, and what such depictions say about our present moment.

One feature that has gone unremarked by critics is the complex way Egan manages a sense of historical authenticity throughout *Manhattan Beach*. As with *The Invisible Circus,* not only does she provide numerous period details and note the backdrop of the war in numerous passages, but also her characters are found to imitate the art they consume. This is particularly the case for Anna, who, as mentioned, is representative of "Bovarysme." Anna is seen reading works by Raymond Chandler and Ellery Queen on numerous occasions, and she even compares her life to the fiction she reads: "Suppose her father hadn't left home at all. Suppose he'd been obliterated by a hail of gangland bullets, Anna's name on his dying lips like 'Rosebud' in *Citizen Kane*? She read an awful lot of Ellery Queens" (106). As a child, Eddie took Anna to see the classic gangster films of the 1930s, such as "*Public Enemy* and *Little Caesar* and *Scarface* (over the disapproving looks of ushers)" (20). Similarly, when she meets Nell, she goes to see *The Glass Key* (1942), the classic noir based on Dashiell Hammett's novel of the same name. Anna's interactions with Dexter, then, are influenced by such works, and later on she considers the mystery of her relationship with Dexter and how it intersects with her father's disappearance as a "deeper story [that] was the mystery that seemed now to have been flashing coded signals at Anna from behind every Agatha Christie and Rex Stout and Raymond Chandler she'd read" (211). She believes her life follows a narrative, that it is a story that is being told. Indeed, part of her motivation to become a diver is that she understands herself through the terms of a melodrama; when she first encounters the misogyny of the lieutenant opposing her diving, she considers: "He was her enemy. It seemed to Anna now that she had always wanted one" (148). Similarly, when her mother leaves for Minnesota to live with her family after Lydia's death, Anna thinks "*This is the end of the story*" (184). Anna's life is constantly distorted by the art she consumes, and she witnesses her life as a story, as a mystery she is trying to solve.

However, Anna's experiences always exceed the generic frameworks that she is so invested in. She also resists the way that life fails to imitate art when she is infatuated with Dexter, as she struggles to reconcile Dexter being both a violent gangster and the man whose "act of kindness" to take Lydia to the beach "had left Anna with one of her happiest memories" (211). Dexter is far more complex than the characters she witnessed in the gangster films she saw as a child. Anna cannot fit these inconsistencies into easy plotlines, and so "she refused. She returned to her book and read herself to sleep" (211). That she stops these thoughts by reading fiction is telling, and this also indicates that Anna uses fiction as an escape as well as a guide. On the day of her first dive, she sees herself as a hero: "Anna often recalled hauling herself up the ladder on test day, triumphant. A moving picture would have ended there, with the promise that, at long last and against all odds, she'd earned the respect of the crusty lieutenant" (289). However, the lieutenant, an inveterate misogynist, "liked her less" (289). That her life fails to live up to the films and books she consumes makes Anna the embodiment of Bovarysme.

While Anna experiences displeasure at life failing to live up to her fictional frames, many reviewers felt that *Manhattan Beach* did not adequately live up to their preconceptions regarding what a historical novel should look like. Egan has indicated the importance of the writings of Damon Runyon, Raymond Chandler, and Harold Q. Masur, as well as many noir films, to the language and atmosphere of *Manhattan Beach* (Schwartz). She cites *On the Waterfront* (1952), the classic noir set on the Brooklyn waterfront, as well as *The Naked City* (1948), as particularly influential (Paul). As Alexandra Schwartz eloquently describes it, such films and books were used to "fix the cadences of the time in her ear." What is interesting is that these noirs are retrospective works, and are nearly works of historical fiction themselves; they are not historical records of the time. Although critics often mention that Egan cites *The Sopranos* as a huge influence on the structure of *Goon Squad*, critics have not yet noted how Tony Soprano serves as a clear influence on Dexter Styles. Amy Clarke explains what Egan took from this show: "The juxtaposition of family-based innocence against mob violence—and the fact that, despite Tony's actions, the viewer still empathizes with him by the end of the episode—demonstrate for Egan a skill in composition and execution to which she aspires."[3] Dexter is remarkably similar: after each night of work where he has sometimes witnessed or participated in some shocking violence, he seeks out his daughter, Tabitha, to watch the sunrise on the dock of his home. Tony Soprano's ability to switch between family man and violent mobster is something that Dexter clearly mirrors, and his growing feeling that his business interests need "legitimacy" is something that is also of constant concern to Tony, the mobster with a therapist (197). Part of the reason for *Manhattan Beach*'s uneasy historicity is that alongside the novel's exhaustive period detail, Egan draws on noir films, as well as contemporary models like Tony Soprano, for the world Dexter Styles inhabits.

Christian Lorentzen particularly focuses his ire on the scenes of organized crime, complaining that "when it comes to the gangsters, Egan is less reliant on research than on the clichés of cinema." While Lorentzen notices that Mr. Q.'s vegetable garden is a reference to Vito Corleone's vegetable garden from *The Godfather,* he fails to recognize that the imagery and language of real-life mobsters has always been drawn from "the clichés of cinema." As mafia expert Federico Varese has pointed out, Al Capone modeled his clothing on The Snapper Kid from the first gangster film, D. W. Griffith's 1912 *The Musketeers of Pig Alley.* Varese also notes that since the 1970s, *The Godfather* "has been a perennial source of inspiration for real-life mobsters." In *The Sopranos*, the members of this organized crime syndicate are constantly watching *The Godfather*—in one scene Tony even lambasts his underlings for watching it so much ("Commendatori"). The images that define the world of organized crime in the popular imagination are a funhouse mirror, where no original version can be ascertained, and to paraphrase Daniel Boorstin, pseudo-events beget further pseudo-events.

This points to a broader argument about the type of historical fiction Egan has produced in *Manhattan Beach*. In Anne Diebel's review, she notes, "Sometimes the novel departs from strict verisimilitude, and in this respect it is less of a conventional historical novel than it at first appears." While Diebel is referring to Anna's dive and some of the other more outlandish scenes in the text, this skirting of verisimilitude also points to the wider way that *Manhattan Beach* is not strictly a historical novel. Whereas I argued that *The Invisible Circus* operates as a form of historiographic metafiction, *Manhattan Beach* is best understood as a pastiche. Pastiche has long been linked with Fredric

Jameson's definitions of postmodernity as an era of "blank parody, a statue with blind eyeballs" (*Postmodernism* 65). Jameson laments the passing of parody, which had a "satiric impulse," while in contrast he conceives of pastiche as "a neutral practice of such mimicry, without any of parody's ulterior motives" (65). In short, he sees political potential in parody, but no possibility for such interventions in the practice of pastiche. However, Egan's text is far from blank mimicry. Rather *Manhattan Beach* can be productively read as representative of Richard Dyer's understanding of pastiche. Dyer suggests that "pastiche does something beyond replication, but not taken to the point that it becomes parody, ridicule or burlesque" (54). In contrast to Jameson, Dyer contends that while pastiche does not have parody's "ulterior motive," this does not mean it is blank or neutral. Dyer states that pastiches occupy an "uncertain, but suggestive and productive, place" (54). *Manhattan Beach,* set during a period of tumultuous changes in relation to class, race, gender, and American global power, exists in this uncertain space, and the novel's drift into numerous genres and forms renders its own historicity uncertain. As Dyer states, a pastiche "selects. It does not reproduce every detail of the referent, but selects a number of traits and makes them the basis of the pastiche" (56). This selection process, based on Egan's exhaustive research, leads to a text based on specific traits of the period, as is evident in how Egan depicts Lydia's disability, Dexter's life of organized crime, and Eddie's seafaring adventures. Viewed in this way, the many critical interpretations that mention the uneasy historicity of the text can be understood as describing Egan's broad pastiche of this historical moment.

Indeed, reading the text as a pastiche enables one to unify many of the readings offered in the issue of *PMLA* dedicated to *Manhattan Beach*. In this issue, three of the critics discuss Egan's depiction of Lydia's disability. Rosemarie Garland-Thomson points out the long tradition of how Lydia is represented, as one of the "always evocative and ever beautiful dying, dead, crippled, comatose, consumptive, or mad mysterious muses—from the Delphic oracle, Sleeping Beauty, Ophelia, Desdemona, Harriet Beecher Stowe's Eva, and Edith Wharton's Lily Bart to all manner of tragic operatic heroines and young female saints" (378). As well as once again connecting Egan's fiction to Wharton's classic—a connection evident in much of Egan's fiction—Garland-Thomson contends that Egan's discussions of disability are part of the "sentimental novelistic tradition," and that "Lydia is an early twentieth-century update of Eva [from *Uncle Tom's Cabin*] redeeming 1930s gangsters just as Eva redeems the 1830s slaveholders" (379). Rachel Adams makes a similar point, but more broadly connects the depictions of disability to the sentimental tradition. Adams notes it is not only Lydia who is depicted this way, but that "many of the men Anna encounters in wartime Manhattan have been declared 4-F, unfit for military service" (368). Similarly, Janet Lyon connects *Manhattan Beach* to the mode of melodrama to explain why Lydia operates as a plot device for the redemption of Dexter, Anna, and Eddie (405). However, like Diebel's suspicion that Egan is doing something "beyond verisimilitude," Lyon also notes that "you begin to suspect Egan of deploying the other, shopworn plots chiefly to authenticate the novel's mid-century ethos, to evoke a moment when the American public tended to perceive disability as hopeless, or tragic, or repulsive" (405). But neither quite label the mode in which Egan is writing; *Manhattan Beach* is a pastiche of the hoary literary devices and plotlines of disability based on the filmic and literary representations of disability that Garland-Thomson, Adams, and Lyon cite. While this does not inculcate her from the criticisms of Garland-Thomson, Adams, and Lyon—Egan self-reproachfully acknowledges that she "enjoyed learning that I'd adhered to shopworn tropes in my approach to physical disability"—there is a broader pastiche aesthetic that defines the uneasy effects that *Manhattan Beach* elicits for many readers ("Academic" 417). As Dyer argues, "pastiche reminds us that a framework is a framework, and also that this is enabling as well as limiting—enabling and setting limits to the exercise of transhistorical sympathy" (177). Egan's depictions of disability are both limited and enabled by her pastiche of the sentimental and melodramatic tropes of the era; for Dyer, pastiche "imitates formal means that are themselves ways of evoking, moulding and eliciting feeling, and thus in the process is able to mobilise feelings even while signalling that it is doing so" (180). Egan's pastiche of the sentimental tradition and melodramas elicits the feelings that were intended at the time; Lyon connects the depiction of Lydia to Dinah Craik's Victorian novel *Olive* (1850), for instance (406), which features a disabled beauty similar to Lydia. Consequently, *Manhattan Beach* is historically accurate in its use of these modes while knowingly acknowledging that they are born of artifice.

Viewing the text as a pastiche also helps navigate Egan's uneasy relationship with fidelity to historical detail and the generic trappings of film noir and seafaring adventures. Egan herself compared Eddie's survival story to "old-fashioned adventure stories" ("Academic" 255). While aboard the ship which is eventually sunk, Eddie's "favorite books were about the sea," and one text he reads is *Death Ship* (1926), a novel by B. Traven about a sea voyage that goes terribly wrong, thus portending what will happen to him and his crew (255). Like Anna's experiences at the shipyard, Eddie's experiences at sea are filtered through the books he reads. Much as the world of organized crime is both cliché-ridden and realistic, Eddie's seafaring adventures are similarly a pastiche of shipwreck fiction. In these moments, Egan clearly draws on Conrad, whose writing, Jameson argues, "float[s] uncertainly somewhere in between Proust and Robert Louis Stevenson" (*Political* 194). It is between similar poles that Egan's text oscillates, of historical exactitude and the generic. Her pastiche of these modes and genres enables her to produce a text of historical fiction that sounds and feels like this era, but Egan uses the form of the historical novel exactly as she uses the Gothic genre in *The Keep*—as a tool to make the text occupy an uncertain place.

The End of the American Century?

In the year *Manhattan Beach* was published, Sam Sacks defined Chabon's *Moonglow,* Whitehead's *The Underground Railroad,* and Saunders's *Lincoln in the Bardo,* alongside Dave Eggers's *Heroes of the Frontier* (2016) and Jonathan Lethem's *A Gambler's Anatomy* (2016), as embodying "the nostalgists aesthetic" (2017). Unmentioned in Sacks's list is the Broadway smash hit *Hamilton* (2015), which sits alongside these works of historical fiction that "imbue stories about America's past with a feel-good vibe." Sacks argues that these novels lack "ambivalence," and fail to "provoke [the] critical thinking and dissent" that he claims "nearly all political fiction" should. While it is patently absurd to claim *The Underground Railroad* in any way creates a "feel-good vibe" about any part of American history, Sacks's broader point about "ambivalence" being missing from these texts is more convincing; they are almost didactic in how they want their readers to respond, whether that is to see Lincoln as the saintly figure Saunders depicts him as, or to admire the intransigent but unwavering genius that Hamilton becomes in Lin Manuel Miranda's production. Sacks demands greater ambivalence during the Trump era and criticizes these writers for practicing escapism from the harsh realities of the present.

As mentioned, while *The Invisible Circus* and *Goon Squad* look at the aftermath of a historical moment, *Manhattan Beach* is a text that, in Allan Hepburn's words, "registers the global 'shifts and realignments' that anticipate the emergence of the United States as a superpower in the 1940s" (385). Indeed, Egan self-consciously pursues this goal, as the phrase "shifts and realignments" is one that Hepburn is quoting from the text (431). As readers in the twenty-first century, we know that the geopolitical dominance of the United States would begin after World War Two, and so the predictions that some characters make about America's place in the world can be judged as either prescient or misinformed. Moreover, the character that Egan chooses to endow with the most foresight is telling. Arthur Berringer, Dexter Styles's father-in-law, is a banker who predicts the rise of America as a global superpower. Like Moose and Thomas Keene in *Look at Me* or Howard in *The Keep,* Arthur is an instance of a character with a "big idea." In a long discussion with Dexter, Arthur acknowledges the failures of the banking system only a few years earlier: "since the Depression, we bankers have had the leisure and . . . solitude, you might say, to think about the future" (91). He notes how previous crises and wars have led to huge changes: "The Civil War left us with a federal government. The Great War made us a creditor nation. As bankers, we must anticipate what changes this war will thrust upon us" (91). While Arthur contends that all crises lead to great changes, what Egan leaves unclear is whether the changes wrought are for the better.

In *The Great Leveler: Violence and the History of Inequality from the Stone Age to the Twenty-First Century,* Walter Scheidel discusses the ways in which inequality has only ever been truly ameliorated by huge events that are impossible to engineer or plan for: "mass mobilization warfare, transformative revolution, state failure, and lethal pandemics" (6). *Manhattan Beach* depicts America on the cusp of one such huge change, one wrought through war and the devastation seen across the globe. Berringer says, "I see the rise of this country to a height no country has occupied, ever. . . . Not the Romans. Not the Carolingians. Not Genghis Khan or the Tatars or Napoleon's France" (91). Pointing ahead to the Marshall Plan, Arthur predicts, "We'll emerge from this war victorious and unscathed, and become bankers to the world. We'll export our dreams, our language, our culture, our way of life. And it will prove irresistible" (92). That Egan has repeated the term "unscathed" as a descriptor in interviews suggests that Arthur is articulating her view of postwar America (Paul). Indeed, it was a period of the seemingly impossible suddenly becoming possible; Dexter realizes when trying to convince Mr. Q. to buy war bonds, "He was tempted to air his suspicion that a newly strengthened United States might use the rule of law to make their way of life extinct. Tammany had already gone—something no one had believed possible" (197). Here, Dexter notes how "Tammany"—short for Tammany Hall, the powerful political entity that dominated New York democratic politics in the first half of the twentieth century—had been decimated by the Depression and was gradually having its influence whittled away further by demographic shifts, numerous strikes, and corruption scandals.[4] This makes Dexter uncertain about his own life, and forces him to consider the possible changes that might happen. Indeed, the unthinkable keeps happening around him, and that is because of the war: "A common enemy had made for strange bedfellows; rumor had it that the great Lucky Luciano had struck a deal with the feds from his jail cell to root out Mussolini sympathizers from the waterfront" (92). Charles "Lucky" Luciano was a real mobster who did inform on fascist sympathizers in exchange for a plea deal over his 1936 conviction for running a prostitution racket (Fisher 60–61). The war has turned their lives upside down; as Anna says of herself, "Her life was a war life; the war *was* her life," meaning they are living through an uncertain but possibly transformative time, much like the mode of pastiche that defines the text (414). Except for the sinking of Eddie's merchant marine vessel by German U-boats, *Manhattan Beach* does not represent any scenes of war directly. Other instances where the war is experienced or shown are peripheral, such as when Anna touches the hull of the USS *Missouri*: "In touching its hull, Anna had touched the war directly for the first time" (298). Almost 300 pages into the novel, this is the first time that a character directly touches America's military might. Here, Anna obliquely experiences the military prowess that would redefine America's place in the globe in the postwar world, a reality that at this point was still unthinkable.

But Arthur does not just talk of financial shifts; he also notes that America will export its "culture." Some of the "shifts and realignments" are hinted at through the behavior of Dexter's children—his sons and his favored daughter, Tabitha. Dexter is perplexed by what his sons get up to: "For reasons that eluded Dexter, his sons liked to enter promotional contests, usually at picture theaters. They tap-danced, turned somersaults, hung from bars upside down, and whistled through their teeth" (84). These twin boys represent the thirst for fame and entertainment which Egan documents in all of her other fiction. There is also Tabitha's vanity: "She was seated at her new vanity, a sixteenth-birthday present. A ring of small electric lightbulbs surrounded its mirror, creating the impression of a Hollywood starlet in her dressing room. What better name for a device that encouraged all the wrong elements of the female personality?" (96). Here, Tabitha's mirror nods ahead to what Egan explores most acutely in *Look at Me*—the gendered nature of the need to be viewed that dominates American life over the second half of the twentieth century, and into the twenty-first. In *Manhattan Beach* Egan looks at the beginnings of the American Century, and consequently the beginnings of the dystopian world she envisions in her earlier fiction in regard to entertainment, image culture, and the vast expansion of the mass media.

In the final section of *Manhattan Beach,* Anna travels across the country to have her baby, Leon, and work in a naval yard on the West Coast. On the way, she watches the release of the USS *Missouri* in the Empress Theater in Vallejo, California, in April 1944 (422). As the boat sets sail, the daughter of Harry Truman fails to break a bottle of champagne on the hull, and this event points ahead to the Truman presidency—Missouri being his home state—which was to begin after the events of *Manhattan Beach*. The *Missouri* is also the ship that is famous for being the site of the Japanese surrender on September 2, 1945. Standing on the harbor, Anna and Eddie watch the San Francisco fog roll in, and the final words of the novel are, "Here it comes" (433). Margaret Cohen argues: "The age of the Anthropocene is in the offing as Anna and Eddie watch the fog roll into San Francisco Bay" (377). And indeed, the beginning of the American Century also portends a vast increase in carbon emissions, the consequences of which Egan explores in the near-future dystopia of *Goon Squad*. The fog could also nod to the atomic bombs about to be dropped on Nagasaki and Hiroshima, and the atomic world that is about to begin. It could also simply embody the uncertain but suggestive future that *Manhattan Beach* points toward; the fog will dissipate and reveal a new postwar order, with huge societal changes at home and the United States dominant abroad. However, Arthur Berringer did put this rise in the context of previous empires—the Romans, the Tatars, and Genghis Khan—all of which have fallen. Consequently, that this fog will roll over and dissipate also points to the 2017 context in which *Manhattan Beach* was published; nine years after the cataclysmic economic crisis and in the first year of the Trump presidency, *Manhattan Beach* looks at the beginnings of the American Century, but it hints that it may have been published toward the end of it. As mentioned, historical fiction often says more about the moment in which it is published than the era it depicts; Egan's historical fiction is not nostalgic, nor is it didactic in the manner of her contemporaries, but rather it resonates with the instability of the present moment.

NOTES

Chapter 1: Understanding Jennifer Egan

1. These terms and trends are described by Adam Kelly, David Harvey, Mark McGurl, Robert McLaughlin, and Theodore Martin, respectively.

2. There are a few notable exceptions to this, namely Martin Paul Eve's *Literature Against Criticism,* Adam Kelly's "Beginning with Postmodernism," and Linda Wagner-Martin's *The Routledge Introduction to American Postmodernism.*

3. She is keen to note that "it had to be re-worked a lot, but there was a germ that went all the way back to college" (von Arbin Ahlander).

4. Since this interview she has taught a class at her alma mater, the University of Pennsylvania, but in literature rather than writing.

5. In a sign of *Emerald City*'s strange publication history—which I delve into in the first chapter—"The Stylist" was in fact published before "One Piece."

Chapter 2: *Emerald City*

1. She is six in the earlier versions, but the accident happened seven years ago. The blurry memories Egan depicts are therefore impossible, an error she corrects in the 1996 edition.

2. Rather than these noted historians, the original says he argued over "Marx and Hegel," a change which demonstrates Egan's dedication to research in her later fiction (54).

Chapter 3: *The Invisible Circus*

1. Egan cites Gitlin's *The Sixties: Years of Hope, Days of Rage* (1987) as an influence. In addition, she says Gitlin's *The Whole World is Watching* (1980) "about the interplay between SDS and the media is something I read in college and that really interested me" (Miller).

2. Martin Paul Eve is, again, a notable exception, as he includes *The Invisible Circus* in his analysis of how Egan depicts academics ("Structural").

3. West offers a comprehensive list of these novels (225–226).

4. The repeated reference to a "leap" Phoebe needs to make, and the fact that "the words 'sickness unto death' [are] drifting through her mind from someplace" after an orgasm later in the novel, suggest the influence of Søren Kierkegaard's philosophies on Egan at this time (275).

5. Similarly, the connection between terrorism and mass media is something that Lessing also depicts in *The Good Terrorist*; after a failed first bombing gets short shrift in the *Guardian* newspaper, a second one is planned.

Chapter 4: *Look at Me*

1. Egan was friends with Wolf in high school (Fradkin).

Chapter 5: *The Keep*

1. Martin Paul Eve connects the structure of *The Invisible Circus* to Todorov's descriptions of how a detective story is structured, so Egan's use of Todorov's theories, or at least the resemblance of her work to Todorov's typologies, is consistent across these texts ("Jennifer Egan").

2. In one of many instances of *The Keep* presaging some of the techniques Egan uses in *A Visit from the Goon Squad,* she proleptically leaps forward to note Rafe died three years later in a car crash (17).

3. When Danny asks Howard whether they are in Germany, Austria, or the Czech Republic, Howard confesses he does not know, as "those borders are constantly sliding around" (4). The questionable location of the castle is therefore another instance of making the reader hesitate, even in regard to where the novel is set.

Chapter 6: *A Visit from the Goon Squad*

1. "X's and O's" was published in both *GQ* and Ken Foster's collection of short stories, *The KGB Bar Reader,* in 1998. In the latter it is titled "X O," and in these earlier versions the details are very different from the one published in *Goon Squad*—for instance, Bennie Salazar is called Jonah Kaplan and has three kids, not one—but the plot, such as the central event of Scotty bringing a fish to the meeting, is the same. Regarding "Forty-Minute Lunch," other than a few minor stylistic changes, there are three larger changes to the later edition: the appendices at the end of the *Harper's* piece become footnotes in the latter version; Jules no longer brags that he has "slept with young actresses . . . and I plan to resume doing so as soon as possible"; and in the 2010 version, a section is added just before Jules sneezes bread everywhere, where he sighs and says to Kitty that the interview is "all such a farce" (92, 175).

2. "X's and O's" was published in *GQ* (1998) and *The KGB Bar Reader* (1998); "The Gold Cure" in *Granta* (2010) and *Men Undressed: Women Writers and The Male Sexual Experience* (2011); "Forty-Minute Lunch" in *Harper's* (1999); "Ask Me If I Care" in *New California Writing* (2011), "Found Objects" (2007) and "Safari" (2010) in the *New Yorker*; "Out of Body" (2010) and "You (Plural)" (2010) in *Tin House*; and "Selling the General" in *This Is Not Chick Lit* (2006).

3. During her keynote address at the *52nd Northeast Modern Language Association Convention* (March 2021), Egan stated her next work is a companion piece to *Goon Squad,* one that focuses on numerous minor characters from *Goon Squad.*

4. *Goon Squad* can indeed be considered part of the body of fiction we know as post-9/11 fiction. There have been numerous essay collections and monographs on this period, but Egan is once again absent from such conversations. For instance, Egan is unmentioned in Georgiana Banita's *Plotting Justice: Narrative Ethics and Literary Culture After 9/11* (2012), Susana Araújo's *Transatlantic Fictions of 9/11 and the War on Terror: Images of Insecurity, Narratives of Captivity* (2015), and Catherine Morley's edited collection *9/11 Topics in Contemporary North American Literature* (2016), to name just a few. Similarly, "Cli-fi" and other awkward monikers have been offered to describe the growing genre of fiction that responds to or depicts the potential effects of climate change. Again, in the criticism on this subject *Goon Squad* is completely absent,

or mentioned only in passing. To name two examples of many, Egan is absent from Adeline Johns-Putra's *Climate Change and the Contemporary Novel* (2019) and only fleetingly mentioned—and then about her relationship to genre—in Pieter Vermeulen's *Literature and the Anthropocene* (2020).

5. Oil operates in the background of other scenes, too. For instance, in "Selling the General," Dolly's New Year's party is disastrous because of the oil which burns so many of the guests. Oil is also the cause of the final scenes of climate change. La Doll's party, as the product of hubris and short-term thinking, points ahead to the post–climate change world Egan envisions in the final chapters.

6. Alex's name is also a mirror of Sasha's—Sasha being a common Eastern European diminutive of Alexander—so their names are another instance of doubling in Egan's fiction.

7. For more on the history of hidden tracks, see Rogers. Hidden tracks have also been a casualty of the digital era, and such tracks are now called "bonus tracks."

Chapter 7: *Manhattan Beach*

1. This is a fictional vessel named after the birth name of Nellie Bly, who sailed around the world in seventy-two days to emulate Jules Verne's character Phileas Fogg from *Around the World in 80 Days* (1873). Bly's achievements nod to the breakthrough of Anna's dive and the gender boundaries that were slowly being dismantled in the first half of the twentieth century (Fessenden).

2. In 2007 Egan wrote an op-ed for the *New York Times* regarding the Atlantic Yards project, and the questionable means by which a project involving "a 22-acre swarm of 16 residential skyscrapers (and a 20,500-seat arena) that would create the densest population swath in the United States" was approved. It is possibly with this development in mind that she wrote the final section of *Goon Squad* ("Developing Story").

3. Clarke is reporting on the moment at the 2014 Birkbeck conference dedicated to Egan's work where an episode of *The Sopranos* was shown.

4. For more on the decline of Tammany Hall, see Fisher 106–107.

WORKS CITED

Works by Jennifer Egan

BOOKS

Emerald City: And Other Stories. Corsair, 2012.

Emerald City: The Collected Works of Jennifer Egan. Picador, 1993.

The Invisible Circus. Anchor, 2007.

The Keep. Anchor, 2007.

Look at Me. Anchor, 2002.

Manhattan Beach. Scribner, 2017.

A Visit from the Goon Squad. Anchor, 2011.

OTHER WRITING

"A Note by Jennifer Egan." *The New Yorker Book of The 60s: Story of a Decade,* edited by Henry Finder, Random House, 2016, pp. 637–639.

"A Thin Line between Mother and Daughter." *Salon,* 14 Nov. 1997, salon.com/1997/11/14/cov_14feature_3/. Accessed 30 Aug. 2020.

"*A Visit from the Goon Squad* by Jennifer Egan – Reading Guide." penguinrandomhouse.com/books/201020/a-visit-from-the-goon-squad-by-jennifer-egan/9780307477477. Accessed 27 Aug. 2020.

"Betrayed but Not Abandoned." *New York Times,* 14 Sept. 1997, movies2.nytimes.com/books/97/09/14/reviews/970914.14eganlt.html.

"Black Box." *New Yorker,* 28 May 2012. https://www.newyorker.com/magazine/2012/06/04/black-box.

"Coming Soon: Jennifer Egan's Black Box.'" *New Yorker,* 23 May 2012. newyorker.com/books/page-turner/coming-soon-jennifer-egans-black-box.

Egan, Jennifer, and George Saunders. *New York Times,* 12 Nov. 2015, "Choose Your Own Adventure: A Conversation with Jennifer Egan and George Saunders." *NYTimes.com,* https://www.nytimes.com/2015/11/15/magazine/choose-your-own-adventure-a-conversation-with-jennifer-egan-and-george-saunders.html. Accessed 30 Aug. 2020.

"Fiction Can Still Do Anything It Wants: Jennifer Egan on Don DeLillo." *Literary Hub,* 3 May 2016, lithub.com/fiction-can-still-do-anything-it-wants-jennifer-egan-on-don-delillo/. Accessed 30 Aug. 2020.

"Forty-Minute Lunch." *Harper's Magazine,* 1 Aug. 1999, harpers.org/archive/1999/08/forty-minute-lunch/. Accessed 30 Aug. 2020.

"Hard Seat." *New Yorker,* 3 June 2019. newyorker.com/magazine/2019/06/10/hard-seat. Accessed 24 Aug. 2020.

"Introduction." *The Best American Short Stories 2014*, edited by Jennifer Egan, Houghton Mifflin Harcourt, 2014, pp. xiii–xix.

"James is a Girl." *New York Times,* 4 Feb. 1996. *NYTimes.com,* nytimes.com/1996/02/04/magazine/james-is-a-girl.html. Accessed 30 Aug. 2020.

"Jennifer Egan: By the Book." *New York Times,* 28 Sept. 2017. *NYTimes.com,* nytimes.com/2017/09/28/books/review/jennifer-egan-by-the-book.html. Accessed 30 Aug. 2020.

"Jennifer Egan To Do." *Guardian,* 22 July 2011. *theguardian.com,* theguardian.com/books/2011/jul/22/jennifer-egan-short-story. Accessed 30 Aug. 2020.

"Jennifer Egan, Writer: 'I Don't Think I've Ever Felt More of a Clear Triumph, a Sense of Finally Having Crossed over a Chasm.'" *New York Magazine,* 11 Jan. 2016, http://nymag.com/news/features/beginnings/jennifer-egan. Accessed 30 Aug. 2020.

"Jennifer Egan's Top Ten List." *Top Ten Books,* 2013, toptenbooks.net/authors/jennifer-egan. Accessed 30 Aug. 2020.

"Keepsake." *The Moment: Wild, Poignant, Life-Changing Stories from 125 Writers and Artists Famous & Obscure,* edited by Larry Smith, Harper Collins, 2012, pp. 196–200.

"Lonely Gay Teen Seeking Same." *New York Times,* 10 Dec. 2000. *NYTimes.com,* nytimes.com/2000/12/10/magazine/lonely-gay-teen-seeking-same.html. Accessed 30 Aug. 2020.

"Love in the Time of No Time." *New York Times,* 23 Nov. 2003. *NYTimes.com,* nytimes.com/2003/11/23/magazine/love-in-the-time-of-no-time.html. Accessed 30 Aug. 2020.

"*Middlemarch*: Jennifer Egan on How George Eliot's Unorthodox Love Life Shaped Her Masterpiece." *Guardian,* 21 Apr. 2018. *Theguardian.com,* theguardian.com/books/2018/apr/21/george-eliot-jennifer-egan-middlemarch-marriage. Accessed 30 Aug. 2020.

"Notes from an Academic Interloper." *PMLA,* vol. 134, no. 2, MLA, 2019, pp. 416–417. *MLA Journals,* doi: 10.1632/pmla.2019.134.2.416.

"Opinion | A Developing Story." *New York Times,* 24 Feb. 2007. *NYTimes.com,* nytimes.com/2007/02/24/opinion/24egan.html. Accessed 30 Aug. 2020.

"Patti Smith at Winterland San Francisco May 13, 1978 Or . . . Boarding House San Francisco August 1979." *The Show I'll Never Forget: 50 Writers Relive Their Most Memorable Concertgoing Experience,* edited by Sean Manning, Da Capo Press, 2007, pp. 103–108.

"Reader, We Married Them." *New York Times,* 4 Apr. 2004. *NYTimes.com,* nytimes.com/2004/04/04/books/reader-we-married-them.html. Accessed 30 Aug. 2020.

"Reading Lucy." *Brooklyn Was Mine,* edited by Chris Knutsen and Valerie Steiker, Penguin, 2008, pp. 21–32.

"The Countess's Private Secretary." *New Yorker,* 29 May 2017. *NewYorker.com,* https://www.newyorker.com/magazine/2017/06/05/the-countess-private-secretary.

"The Thin Red Line." *New York Times,* 27 July 1997. *NYTimes.com,* nytimes.com/1997/07/27/magazine/the-thin-red-line.html. Accessed 30 Aug. 2020.

"Uniforms in the Closet." *New York Times,* 28 June 1998. *NYTimes.com,* nytimes.com/1998/06/28/magazine/uniforms-in-the-closet.html. Accessed 30 Aug. 2020.

"Weinberger v. Wiesenfeld (1975)." *Fight of the Century: Writers Reflect on 100 Years of Landmark ACLU Cases,* edited by Michael Chabon and Ayelet Waldman, Avid Reader Press, 2020, pp. 152–157.

"Why a Priest." *New York Times,* 4 Apr. 1999. *NYTimes.com*, nytimes.com/1999/04/04/magazine/why-a-priest.html. Accessed 30 Aug. 2020.

Secondary Sources

"The 100 Best Books of the 21st Century." *Guardian,* 21 Sept. 2019. *theguardian.com,* theguardian.com/books/2019/sep/21/best-books-of-the-21st-century. Accessed 25 Aug. 2020.

Adams, Rachel. "Siblings, Disability, Genre in Jennifer Egan's *Manhattan Beach*." *PMLA,* vol. 134, no. 2, 2019, pp. 366–371. *MLA Journals,* doi: 10.1632/pmla.2019.134.2.366

Alford, Robert. "Celebrating the Possibilities of Fiction: A Conversation with Jennifer Egan." *PopMatters,* 20 Feb. 2012, popmatters.com/154523-celebrating-the-possibilities-of-fiction-a-conversation-with-jennife-2495885422.html. Accessed 30 August 2020.

Araújo, Susana. *Transatlantic Fictions of 9/11 and the War on Terror: Images of Insecurity, Narratives of Captivity*. Bloomsbury Academic, 2017.

Banita, Georgiana. *Plotting Justice: Narrative Ethics & Literary Culture after 9/11*. University of Nebraska Press, 2012.

Barthes, Roland. *Camera Lucida: Reflections on Photography*. Translated by Richard Howard. Vintage, 2000.

Baudrillard, Jean. *Simulacra and Simulation*. Translated by Sheila Faria Glaser. The University of Michigan Press, 1994.

Beckman, Jamie. "In Defense of Chick Lit." *The Frisky*. 26 May 2017, web.archive.org/web/20170526154404/http:/thefrisky.com/2011-04-19/in-defense-of-chick-lit/. Accessed 30 Aug. 2020.

Birnbaum, Robert. "Jennifer Egan." *The Morning News,* 18 Aug. 2010, themorningnews.org/article/jennifer-egan. Accessed 25 Aug. 2020.

Blair, J. H. *The Good Parts: The Best Erotic Writing in Modern Fiction*. Berkley Books, 2000.

Boorstin, Daniel. *The Image: A Guide to Pseudo-Events in America*. First Vintage, 1991.

Boxall, Peter. *Twenty-First-Century Fiction: A Critical Introduction*. Cambridge UP, 2013.

Boyle, David. *Authenticity: Brands, Fakes, Spin and the Lust for Real Life*. Harper Perennial, 2003.

Brooks, Adam, director. *The Invisible Circus*. Fine Line Features, Industry Entertainment, Nicolas Entertainment, 2001.

Brown, Nicholas. *Autonomy: The Social Ontology of Art under Capitalism*. Duke UP, 2019.

Butchard, Dorothy. "Jennifer Egan." *The Routledge Companion to Twenty-First Century Literary Fiction,* edited by Daniel O'Gorman and Robert Eaglestone, Routledge, 2019, pp. 360–371.

Campoy, Ana. "More than 60% of Donald Trump's Twitter Followers Look Suspiciously Fake." *Quartz,* October 12, 2018. qz.com/1422395/how-many-of-donald-trumps-twitter-followers-are-fake/. Accessed 26 Aug. 2020.

Chamberlin, Jeremiah. "Jennifer Egan." *Glimmer Train,* glimmertrain.com/bulletins/essays/b137egan.php. Accessed 30 Aug. 2020.

Charles, Ron. "Jennifer Egan's '*A Visit from the Goon Squad*.'" *The Washington Post,*

16 June 2010, http://washingtonpost.com/wp-dyn/content/article/2010/06/15/AR2010061504751.html. Accessed 30 Aug. 2020.

Christie's. "Egan, Jennifer (b. 1962). *A Visit from the Goon Squad.*" christies.com/lotfinder/lot_details.aspx?intObjectID=5847690. Accessed 27 Aug. 2020.

Ciabattari, Jane. "Jennifer Egan Interview, *A Visit from the Goon Squad.*" *The Daily Beast,* 29 June 2010, thedailybeast.com/articles/2010/06/29/jennifer-egan-interview-a-visit-from-the-goon-squad. Accessed 30 Aug. 2020.

Clarke, Amy. "A Visit from Jennifer Egan." *Center for Contemporary Literature, Birkbeck, University of London,* 2015, http://www.ccl.bbk.ac.uk/a-visit-from-jennifer-egan/. Accessed 1 Sept. 2020.

Cohen, Margaret. "A Feminist Plunge into Sea Knowledge." *PMLA,* vol. 134, no. 2, 2019, pp. 372–377. *MLA Journals,* doi: 10.1632/pmla.2019.134.2.372.

"Commendatori." *The Sopranos.* Chase Films, Brad Grey Television, 2000.

Conrad, Joseph. *Lord Jim.* Signet Classics, 2000.

Cooke, Rachel. "Jennifer Egan: 'I Was Never a Hot, Young Writer. But Then I Had a Quantum Leap.'" *The Observer,* 24 Sept. 2017, theguardian.com/books/2017/sep/24/jennifer-egan-quantum-leap-manhattan-beach-visit-from-the-goon-squad. Accessed 30 Aug. 2020.

Cowart, David. *The Tribe of Pyn: Literary Generations in the Postmodern Period.* University of Michigan Press, 2015.

Dames, Nicholas. "Seventies Throwback Fiction." *N+1,* Winter 2015, nplusonemag.com/issue-21/reviews/seventies-throwback-fiction/. Accessed 30 Aug. 2020.

———. "The Theory Generation." *N+1,* Summer 2012, nplusonemag.com/issue-14/reviews/the-theory-generation/. Accessed 30 Aug. 2020.

DeLillo, Don. *Mao II.* Jonathan Cape, 1991.

Diebel, Anne. "Anna Papa Mama Liddy." *London Review of Books,* vol. 39, no. 23, Nov. 2017. *lrb.co.uk,* lrb.co.uk/the-paper/v39/n23/anne-diebel/anna-papa-mama-liddy.

Dinnen, Zara. *The Digital Banal: New Media and American Literature and Culture.* Columbia UP, 2018.

———. "'This Is All Artificial': An Interview with Jennifer Egan." *Post45,* vol. 20, 2016. post45.org/2016/05/this-is-all-artificial-an-interview-with-jennifer-egan/.

Draper, Robert. "The Man Behind the President's Tweets." *New York Times,* 16 Apr. 2018. nytimes.com/2018/04/16/magazine/dan-scavino-the-secretary-of-offense.html.

Dubrow, Heather. *Genre.* Methuen, 1982.

Duvall, John. "Historical Fiction." *American Literature in Transition 1990–2000,* edited by Stephen J. Burn, Cambridge UP, pp. 124–139.

Dyer, Richard. *Pastiche.* Routledge, 2007.

Edgar, Deidre. "Book Award: Did Egan Win, or Did Franzen Lose?" *LA Times,* 15 Mar. 2011, latimesblogs.latimes.com/readers/2011/03/book-award-did-egan-win-or-did-franzen-lose.html. Accessed 30 Aug. 2020.

Edwards, Caroline. "The Networked Novel." *The Routledge Companion to Twenty-First Century Literary Fiction,* edited by Daniel O'Gorman and Robert Eaglestone, Routledge, 2019, pp, 13–24.

English, T. J. *Paddy Whacked: The Untold Story of the Irish American Gangster.* Harper Collins, 2005.

Eve, Martin Paul. "Jennifer Egan." *Dictionary of Literary Biography: Twenty-First-Century American Novelists,* edited by George Parker Anderson, Gale, 2018, pp. 75–86.

———. *Literature Against Criticism: University English and Contemporary Fiction in Conflict*. Open Book Publishers, 2016.

———. "'Structural Dissatisfaction': Academics on Safari in the Novels of Jennifer Egan." *Open Library of Humanities,* vol. 1, no. 1, *Open Library of Humanities,* 2015, pp. 1–24. doi: 10.16995/olh.29.

———. "Textual Scholarship and Contemporary Literary Studies: Jennifer Egan's Editorial Processes and the Archival Edition of *Emerald City*." *Lit: Literature Interpretation Theory,* vol. 31, no. 1, *Taylor & Francis,* 2020, pp. 25–41. doi: 10.1080/10436928.2020.1709713.

Fessenden, Marissa. "Nellie Bly's Record-Breaking Trip Around the World Was, to Her Surprise, A Race." *Smithsonian Magazine,* smithsonianmag.com/smart-news/nellie-blys-record-breaking-trip-around-world-was-to-her-surprise-race-180957910/. Accessed 29 Aug. 2020.

Fisher, James. *On the Irish Waterfront: The Crusader, the Movie, and the Soul of the Port of New York*. Cornell University Press, 2011.

Fradkin, Lori. "Off the Shelf: Jennifer Egan." *New York Magazine,* nymag.com/arts/books/features/19359/. Accessed 24 Aug. 2020.

Funk, Wolfgang. "Found Objects: Narrative (as) Reconstruction in Jennifer Egan's *A Visit from the Goon Squad*." *The Aesthetics of Authenticity: Medial Constructions of the Real,* edited by Wolfgang Funk, Florian Gross, and Irmtraud Huber, Transaction, 2012, pp. 41–61.

Garland-Thomson, Rosemarie. "Representing the Erotic Life of Disabled Women: Jennifer Egan's *Manhattan Beach* and Anne Finger's *A Woman, in Bed*." *PMLA,* vol. 134, no. 2, MLA, 2019, pp. 378–383. *MLA Journals*. doi: 10.1632/pmla.2019.134.2.378.

Gibbons, Alison. "Postmodernism Is Dead. What Comes next?" *TLS,* 12 Jun. 2017, the-tls.co.uk/articles/postmodernism-dead-comes-next/. Accessed 28 Aug. 2020.

Gitlin, Todd. *The Sixties: Years of Hope, Days of Rage*. Random House Publishing Group, 2013.

———. *The Whole World Is Watching: Mass Media in the Making and Unmaking of the New Left*. University of California Press, 2003.

Goffman, Ervin. *The Presentation of Self in Everyday Life*. Doubleday, 1959.

Harvey, David. *A Brief History of Neoliberalism*. Oxford UP, 2007.

Hayles, N. Katherine. *How We Became Posthuman: Virtual Bodies in Cybernetics, Literature, and Informatics*. University of Chicago Press, 2008.

Hepburn, Allan. "Vanishing Worlds: Epic Disappearance in 'Manhattan Beach.'" *PMLA,* vol. 134, no. 2, MLA, 2019, pp. 384–390. *MLA Journals*. doi: 10.1632/pmla.2019.134.2.384.

Herbert, Brian. *The Forgotten Heroes: The Heroic Story of the United States Merchant Marine*. Tom Doherty Associates, 2005.

"Here Are EW's Top 10 Fiction Books of the Decade." *EW.Com,* ew.com/books/2019/11/25/best-of-the-decade-top-10-fiction-books/. Accessed 27 Aug. 2020.

Hoberek, Andrew. "Introduction: After Postmodernism." *Twentieth Century Literature,* vol. 53, no. 3, 2007, pp. 233–247. *JSTOR,* jstor.org/stable/20479812.

Hogan, Ron. "The Beatrice Interview: Jennifer Egan." *Beatrice,* 2001, http://beatrice.com/wordpress/interview-jennifer-egan/. Accessed 30 Aug. 2020.

Hogle, Jerrold. "Introduction: The Gothic in Western Culture." *The Cambridge Companion to Gothic Fiction,* edited by Jerrold Hogle, Cambridge UP, 2002, pp. 1–20.

———. "Introduction: Modernity and The Proliferation of The Gothic." *The*

Cambridge Companion to the Modern Gothic, edited by Jerrold Hogle, Cambridge UP, 2014, pp. 3–19.
Huehls, Mitchum. "Historical Fiction and the End of History." *American Literature in Transition 2000–2010,* edited by Rachel Greenwald Smith, Cambridge UP, 2017, pp. 138–151.
Hughes, Evan. *Literary Brooklyn: The Writers of Brooklyn and the Story of American City Life.* Henry Holt and Company, 2011.
Hutcheon, Linda. *A Poetics of Postmodernism: History, Theory, Fiction.* Routledge, 1988.
Hutchinson, George. "A Historicist Novel." *PMLA,* vol. 134, no. 2, MLA, 2019, pp. 391–397. *MLA Journals.* doi: 10.1632/pmla.2019.134.2.391.
Isaacson, Walter. *Steve Jobs.* Simon and Schuster, 2011.
Itzkoff, Dave. "Jennifer Egan Discusses TV Plans for '*A Visit from the Goon Squad.*'" *ArtsBeat,* 21 Apr. 2011, artsbeat.blogs.nytimes.com/2011/04/21/jennifer-egan-talks-tv-plans-for-a-visit-from-the-goon-squad/.
Jack, Jordynn. "Gender and Wartime Work." *PMLA,* vol. 134, no. 2, 2019, pp. 398–404. *MLA Journals.* doi: 10.1632/pmla.2019.134.2.398.
Jameson, Fredric. *The Political Unconscious: Narrative as a Socially Symbolic Act.* Routledge Classics, 2002.
———, *Postmodernism, Or, The Cultural Logic of Late Capitalism.* Duke UP, 1991.
Johns-Putra, Adeline. *Climate Change and the Contemporary Novel.* 2019.
Johnston, Katherine. "Metadata, Metafiction, and the Stakes of Surveillance in Jennifer Egan's *A Visit from the Goon Squad.*" *American Literature,* vol. 89, no. 1, 2017, pp. 155–184. *uci.primo.exlibrisgroup.com,* doi:10.1215/00029831-3788753.
Kachka, Boris. "*A Visit from the Goon Squad* Author Jennifer Egan on Reaping Awards and Dodging Literary Feuds." *Vulture,* 11 May 2011, vulture.com/2011/05/jennifer_egan_goon_squad_inter.html. Accessed 24 Aug. 2020.
Kaufman, Leslie. "Without Any Fanfare, Jennifer Egan Switches Publishers." *Media Decoder Blog,* 18 Dec. 2012, mediadecoder.blogs.nytimes.com/2012/12/18/without-any-fanfare-jennifer-egan-switches-publishers/. Accessed 24 Aug. 2020.
Kelly, Adam. "Beginning with Postmodernism." *Twentieth-Century Literature,* vol. 57, no. 3–4, Dec. 2011, pp. 391–422. *Duke UP,* doi:10.1215/0041462X-2011-4009.
———. "The New Sincerity." *Postmodern/Postwar and After,* edited by Jason Gladstone, Andrew Hoberek, and Daniel Worden. University of Iowa Press, 2016, pp. 197–208.
Kirby, Alan. *Digimodernism: How New Technologies Dismantle the Postmodern and Reconfigure Our Culture.* A&C Black, 2009.
Kois, Dan. "Why Do Writers Abandon Novels?" *New York Times,* 4 Mar. 2011. *NYTimes.com,* nytimes.com/2011/03/06/books/review/Kois-t.html. Accessed 24 Aug. 2020.
Konstantinou, Lee. *Cool Characters: Irony and American Fiction.* Harvard UP, 2016.
Lacan, Jacques. *Ecrits: A Selection.* Translated by Bruce Fink, W. W. Norton & Company, 2004.
La Force, Thessaly. "Jennifer Egan Fever." *The Paris Review,* 12 July 2011, theparisreview.org/blog/2011/07/12/jennifer-egan-fever/. Accessed 24 Aug. 2020.
Lambert, Stephanie. "'The Real Dark Side, Baby': New Sincerity and Neoliberal Aesthetics in David Foster Wallace and Jennifer Egan." *Critique: Studies in Contemporary Fiction,* Taylor & Francis, 2020, pp. 1–18. doi: 10.1080/00111619.2020.1727831.
Lessing, Doris. *The Good Terrorist.* Knopf Doubleday, 2010.

Lopate, Leonard. “Jennifer Egan Returns With ‘*Manhattan Beach*.’” 4 Oct. 2017. *WNYC,* wnyc.org/story/jennifer-egan/. Accessed 25 Aug. 2020.

Lorentzen, Christian. “Jennifer Egan’s Strained New World War II Novel.” *Vulture,* 28 Sept. 2017, vulture.com/2017/09/jennifer-egans-strained-new-world-war-ii-novel.html. Accessed 30 Aug. 2020.

Lukin, Joshua. “Part of Us That Can’t Be Touched.” *Guernica,* 1 July 2010, guernicamag.com/egan_7_1_10/. Accessed 30 Aug. 2020.

Lyon, Janet. “The Wheelchair: A Three-Part Drama.” *PMLA,* vol. 134, no. 2, 2019, pp. 405–411. *MLA Journals,* doi: 10.1632/pmla.2019.134.2.405.

MacCannell, Dean. *The Ethics of Sightseeing*. University of California Press, 2011.

———. “Staged Authenticity: Arrangements of Social Space in Tourist Settings.” *American Journal of Sociology,* vol. 79, no. 3, 1973, pp. 589–603, *JSTOR,* https://www.jstor.org/stable/2776259.

———. *The Tourist: A New Theory of the Leisure Class*. University of California Press, 2013.

———. “Why It Never Really Was About Authenticity.” *Society,* vol. 45, no. 4, Springer Nature, July 2008, pp. 334–37. *EBSCOhost,* doi:10.1007/s12115-008-9110-8.

Mak, Aaron, “Trump Was Losing Twitter Followers Until He Incited a Riot.” *Slate.com,* 12 January 2021. https://slate.com/technology/2021/01/trump-twitter-ban-followers-capitol-riot.html. Accessed 11 March 2021.

Maren, Michael, director. *A Short History of Decay*. Big Fan Films, Short History, 2015.

Martin, Theodore. *Contemporary Drift: Genre, Historicism, and the Problem of the Present*. Columbia UP, 2017.

Masterson, John. “‘It’s Not Dark Yet, but It’s Getting There’: Listening for the End Times in the Contemporary American Novel.” *Studia Neophilologica,* vol. 88, no. sup1, Mar. 2016, pp. 68–80. *Taylor and Francis,* doi:10.1080/00393274.2015.1096043.

McGurl, Mark. *The Program Era: Postwar Fiction and the Rise of Creative Writing*. Harvard UP, 2009.

McLaughlin, Robert L. “Post-Postmodern Discontent: Contemporary Fiction and the Social World.” *Symplokē,* vol. 12, no. 1/2, University of Nebraska Press, 2004, pp. 53–68. *JSTOR,* jstor.org/stable/40550666.

Melville, Herman. *Moby-Dick*. Wordsworth Classics, 2002.

Merrick, Elizabeth. *This Is Not Chick Lit: Original Stories by America’s Best Women Writers*. Random House Trade Paperbacks, 2006.

Messud, Claire. “Emerald City. (Book).” *Times Literary Supplement,* no. 4702, Times Supplements Ltd, 1993, p. 24. *Gale*, link.gale.com/apps/doc/H1100109632/LitRC?u=ucirvine&sid=LitRC&xid=f3cb9fbe.

Michod, Alec. “The Rumpus Interview with Jennifer Egan.” *The Rumpus.Net,* 23 June 2010, therumpus.net/2010/06/the-rumpus-interview-with-jennifer-egan/. Accessed 30 Aug. 2020.

Miller, Laura. “Face Value.” *Salon,* 15 Nov. 2001, salon.com/2001/11/14/egan_2/. Accessed 30 Aug. 2020.

Miranda, Lin-Manuel. *Hamilton*. Walt Disney Pictures, 2020.

Mishra, Pankaj. “Modernity’s Undoing.” *London Review of Books,* vol. 33, no. 07, Mar. 2011. *lrb.co.uk,* lrb.co.uk/the-paper/v33/n07/pankaj-mishra/modernity-s-undoing.

Moling, Martin. “‘No Future’: Time, Punk Rock and Jennifer Egan’s *A Visit from the Goon Squad*.” *Arizona Quarterly: A Journal of American Literature, Culture, and Theory,* vol. 72, no. 1, Johns Hopkins UP, Mar. 2016, pp. 51–77. *Project MUSE,* doi:10.1353/arq.2016.0000.

Moran, Alexander. "The Genrefication of Contemporary American Fiction." *Textual Practice,* vol. 33, no. 2, Feb. 2019, pp. 229–44. *Taylor and Francis,* doi:10.1080/0950236X.2018.1509272.

Morley, Catherine, editor. *9/11: Topics in Contemporary North American Literature.* Bloomsbury Publishing, 2016.

Nealon, Jeffrey. *Post-Postmodernism: Or, The Cultural Logic of Just-in-Time Capitalism.* Stanford UP, 2012.

Newman, Daniel Aureliano. "Your Body Is Our Black Box: Narrating Nations in Second-Person Fiction by Edna O'Brien and Jennifer Egan." *Frontiers of Narrative Studies,* vol. 4, no. 1, June 2018, pp. 42–65. *degruyter.com,* doi:10.1515/fns-2018-0004.

North, Anna. "Jonathan Franzen Loses Book Award to Some Lady." *Jezebel,* jezebel.com/jonathan-franzen-loses-book-award-to-some-lady-5781688. Accessed 18 Aug. 2020.

Ohlson, Karen. "Jennifer Egan: 'I Needed to Let Go of Chronology.'" *Talking Writing.* 13 June 2011, http://talkingwriting.com/jennifer-egan-%E2%80%9Ci-needed-to-let-go-of-chronology%E2%80%9D.

Olson, Daniel. "Renovation is Hell, and Other Gothic Truths Inside Jennifer Egan's *The Keep.*" *21st-Century Gothic: Great Gothic Novels Since 2000,* edited by Daniel Olson, Scarecrow Press, 2010, pp. 327–341.

Paul, Pamela. "Jennifer Egan Talks About *Manhattan Beach.*" *The Book Review,* 6 Oct. 2017. *New York Times,* www.nytimes.com/2017/10/06/books/review/jennifer-egan-talks-about-manhattan-beach.html. Accessed 29 Aug. 2020.

Preece, Julian. *Baader-Meinhof and the Novel: Narratives of the Nation, Fantasies of the Revolution, 1970-2010.* Palgrave Macmillan, 2012.

Prinz, Jesse. "The Aesthetics of Punk Rock: Punk Music Aesthetics Identity Taste." *Philosophy Compass,* vol. 9, no. 9, Sept. 2014, *Wiley,* pp. 583–93. doi:10.1111/phc3.12145.

Proust, Marcel. *Swann's Way: In Search of Lost Time, Volume 1 (Penguin Classics Deluxe Edition).* Penguin, 2004.

Reilly, Charlie. "An Interview with Jennifer Egan." *Contemporary Literature,* vol. 50, no. 3, University of Wisconsin Press, 2009, pp. 439–60. *Project MUSE,* doi:10.1353/cli.0.0074.

Rogers, Jude. "Manna for Fans: The History of the Hidden Track in Music." *The Observer,* 25 Jan. 2015. *www.theguardian.com,* https://www.theguardian.com/music/2015/jan/25/history-hidden-tracks-musicians-albums. Accessed 30 Aug. 2020.

Rousselot, Elodie. "Introduction: Exoticizing the Past in Contemporary Neo-Historical Fiction." *Exoticizing the Past in Contemporary Neo-Historical Fiction,* edited by Elodie Rousselot, Springer, 2014, pp. 1–16.

Sacks, Sam. "They Could Be Heroes." *The New Republic,* Mar. 2017. *The New Republic,* newrepublic.com/article/140954/nostalgic-fiction-booming-eggers-chabon-lethem.

Scanlan, Margaret. *Plotting Terror: Novelists and Terrorists in Contemporary Fiction.* University of Virginia Press, 2001.

Scheidel, Walter. *The Great Leveler: Violence and the History of Inequality from the Stone Age to the Twenty-First Century.* Princeton UP, 2018.

Schwartz, Alexandra. "Jennifer Egan's Travels Through Time." *New Yorker,* newyorker.com/magazine/2017/10/16/jennifer-egans-travels-through-time. Accessed 25 Aug. 2020.

Sedgwick, Eve Kosofsky. *The Coherence of Gothic Conventions*. Methuen, 1986.

Shields, David. *Reality Hunger*. Knopf Doubleday Publishing Group, 2010.

Smith, Jennifer J. *American Short Story Cycle*. Edinburgh UP, 2017.

Smith, Rachel Greenwald. "Six Propositions on Compromise Aesthetics." *The Account: A Journal of Prose, Poetry, and Thought*. Fall 2014, https://theaccountmagazine.com/article/six-propositions-on-compromise-aesthetics.

Stanley, Jodee. "Emerald City." *Ploughshares,* vol. 22, no. 1, Ploughshares, Inc., 1996, pp. 205–207.

Steinberg, Julie. "Jennifer Egan on Winning the 2011 Pulitzer Prize for Fiction." *WSJ,* 18 Apr. 2011, blogs.wsj.com/speakeasy/2011/04/18/jennifer-egan-on-winning-the-2011-pulitzer-prize-for-fiction/. Accessed 25 Aug. 2020.

Szalay, Michael. "The Author as Executive Producer." *Neoliberalism and Contemporary Literary Culture,* edited by Mitchum Huehls and Rachel Greenwald Smith, Johns Hopkins UP, 2017, pp. 255–276.

Sze, Sarah. *Triple Point,* edited by Holly Block and Carey Lovelace, Gregory R. Miller and Company, 2013.

Tillotson, Kristin. "A Very Goon Year for Jennifer Egan." *Star Tribune,* 6 Sept. 2011, https://www.startribune.com/a-very-goon-year-for-jennifer-egan/128426023/. Accessed 30 Aug. 2020.

Todorov, Tzvetan. *The Fantastic: A Structural Approach to a Literary Genre*. Translated by Richard Howard, Cornell UP, 1975.

Truffin, Sherry R. "Creation Anxiety in Gothic Metafiction: *The Dark Half* and *Lunar Park*." *A Companion to American Gothic,* edited by Charles L. Crow, John Wiley & Sons, 2013, pp, 56–68.

Varese, Frederico. "Mafia at the Movies." *Times Literary Supplement,* the-tls.co.uk/articles/mafia-movies-varese/. Accessed 29 Aug. 2020.

Vermeulen, Pieter. *Literature and the Anthropocene*. Routledge. 2020.

Vida, Vendela. "An Interview with Jennifer Egan." *Believer Magazine,* 1 Aug. 2006, believermag.com/an-interview-with-jennifer-egan/. Accessed 25 Aug. 2020.

von Arbin Ahlander, Astri. "Jennifer Egan." *The Days of Yore,* 19 Apr. 2011, http://thedaysofyore.com/2011/jennifer-egan/. Accessed 25 Aug. 2020.

Vorda, Allan. "Habit of Mind: An Interview with Jennifer Egan." *Rain Taxi,* 2018. raintaxi.com/habit-of-mind-an-interview-with-jennifer-egan/. Accessed 25 Aug. 2020.

Wagner-Martin, Linda. *The Routledge Introduction to American Postmodernism*. Routledge, 2019.

Wallace, David Foster. *A Supposedly Fun Thing I'll Never Do Again*. Little, Brown Book Group, 2012.

Wallace-Wells, David. *The Uninhabitable Earth: Life After Warming*. Crown, 2019.

Walpole, Horace. *The Castle of Otranto: A Gothic Story*. Oxford UP, 1998.

West, Mark. "The Contemporary Sixties Novel: Post-Postmodernism and Historiographic Metafiction." *21st Century US Historical Fiction,* edited by Ruth Maxey, 2020, pp. 209–227.

Wexler, Michael, and John Hulme. *Voices of the Xiled: A Generation Speaks for Itself*. Main Street Books, 1994.

Wharton, Edith. *The House of Mirth*. Simon and Schuster, 2020.

Williams, Jeffrey J. "Generation Jones and Contemporary US Fiction." *American Literary History,* vol. 28, no. 1, Oxford UP, 2016, pp. 94–122. doi: 10.1093/alh/ajv052.

Witt, John Fabian. "Jennifer Egan's Dive for the Inarticulate." *PMLA*, vol. 134, no. 2, MLA, 2019, pp. 412–415. doi: 10.1632/pmla.2019.134.2.412.

Wolf, Naomi. *The Beauty Myth: How Images of Beauty Are Used Against Women.* Harper Collins, 2009.

Wylot, David. *Reading Contingency: The Accident in Contemporary Fiction*. Routledge, 2019.

Yabroff, Jennie. "Hearing Voices: In *The Keep,* Jennifer Egan Stakes Out New Territory." *SFGate,* 23 July 2006, sfgate.com/living/article/Hearing-voices-In-The-Keep-Jennifer-Egan-2492384.php. Accessed 30 Aug. 2020.

Zappen, James P. "Affective Identification in Jennifer Egan's *A Visit from the Goon Squad.*" *Lit: Literature Interpretation Theory,* vol. 27, no. 4, 2016, pp. 294–309. *uci.primo.exlibrisgroup.com,* doi:10.1080/10436928.2016.1236519.

Zuboff, Shoshana. *The Age of Surveillance Capitalism: The Fight for a Human Future at the New Frontier of Power*. Public Affairs, 2019.

INDEX